Spiritualism
and
Occultism

Books by Dion Fortune with Gareth Knight
The Magical Battle of Britain
An Introduction to Ritual Magic
The Circuit of Force
Principles of Hermetic Philosophy
Spiritualism and Occultism

Future titles
Sane Occultism
Practical Occultism
Mystical Meditations on the Collects

Other books by Dion Fortune
Applied Magic
Aspects of Occultism
Glastonbury - Avalon of the Heart
Machinery of the Mind
Psychic Self-Defence
The Cosmic Doctrine
The Esoteric Orders and their Work
The Esoteric Philosophy of Love and Marriage
The Mystical Qabalah
The Problem of Purity
The Psychology of the Servant Problem
The Soya Bean
The Training and Work of an Initiate
Through the Gates of Death

Occult Fiction
The Secrets of Dr Taverner
The Demon Lover
The Goat-Foot God
The Winged Bull
The Sea Priestess
Moon Magic

Other books by Gareth Knight
A Practical Guide to Qabalistic Symbolism
Esoteric Training in Everyday Life
Evoking the Goddess (*aka* The Rose Cross and the Goddess)
Experience of the Inner Worlds
Magic and the Western Mind (*aka* A History of White Magic)
Magical Images and the Magical Imagination
Merlin and the Grail Tradition
Occult Exercises and Practices
Tarot and Magic (*aka* The Treasure House of Images)
The Secret Tradition in Arthurian Legend
The Magical World of the Inklings
The Magical World of the Tarot
The Occult: an Introduction
The Practice of Ritual Magic

SPIRITUALISM
AND
OCCULTISM
by
Dion Fortune

with commentary edited by
Gareth Knight

THOTH PUBLICATIONS
Loughborough, Leicestershire.

Copyright ©1999 The Society of the Inner Light
Copyright©1999 Gareth Knight

All rights reserved. No reproduction, copy or transmission of this publication may be made without written permission. No paragraph of this publication may be reproduced, copied or transmitted save with written permission or in accordance with the provision of the Copyright Act 1956 (as amended). Any person who does any unauthorised act in relation to this publication may be liable to criminal prosecution and civilclaims for damages.

The Moral Rights of the Authors have been asserted.

Dion Fortune™ is a registered trademark.

Details of the "Work and Aims" of the Society of the Inner Light, founded by Dion Fortune, may be obtained by writing (with postage please) to the Secretariat at
38 Steele's Road, London NW3 4RG

A CIP catalogue record for this book is available from the British Library.

Cover design by Rebecca Mazonowicz

Printed and bound in Great Britain

Published by Thoth Publications
64 Leopold Street, Loughborough, LE11 5DN
First published 1999

ISBN 1 870450 38 8

CONTENTS

PART ONE

Spiritualism and Occultism in Practice   10
    Spiritualism in the Light of Occult Science   10
    Communication with the Departed   16
    Spirit-teaching and Reincarnation   20

Commentary   28
    Desirable Conditions for Trance Mediumship   30
    Modus Operandi of Trance Communication   31
    Séance Transcript of November 26th 1941   33
    The Secret Tradition: Occultism and Spiritualism   41
    The Secret Tradition: The Occult Movement Today   44
    The Secret Tradition: The Method of Occult Science   47
    Interview with "White Wing"   50
    The Fraternity of the Inner Light and Spiritualism   58

PART TWO

The Psychology, Phenomena and Technique of Trance   63
    The Psychology of Trance Mediumship   63
    The Physical Phenomena of Trance   69
    The Mental Phenomena of Trance   72
    Trance and Hypnosis   75
    The Technique of Trance   79

Commentary   86
    The Problem of Trance   86
    How Trance Communication is Made   92
    Sitting of February 8th, 1921   98
    The Technique of Trance   102

PART THREE

Inhabitants of the Unseen   116
    Souls of the Departed   116
    Projections of the Living   118
    Angelic Hierarchies   119
    Elementals   120
    Nature Spirits   122
    The Qlipphoth or Demons   123
    Thought Forms   124

Commentary   128
    Who are the Masters?   128
    Teachings of the Masters   136
    Contacts with David Carstairs   147

PART FOUR

The Psychology of Psychic and Higher Consciousness   157
    Clairvoyance   157
    Astral Psychism   161
    The Psychology of Clairvoyance   164
    The Real Nature of Vision   169
    Consciousness of the Planes   172
    The Dawn of the Higher Consciousness   174

Commentary   179
    Psychology and Occultism   180

Introduction

The main text of this work by Dion Fortune first appeared as articles in "The Inner Light" magazine in 1929 and 1930, and was later published in volume form, under the title of "Spiritualism in the Light of Occult Science."

My own contribution has been to bring to light related writings by Dion Fortune, some not published before, or available only in small magazines, and to group them in the form of Commentaries loosely linked by me. This book should thus form a valuable record of Dion Fortune's unique first hand experience of mediumship and its use in the occult world, and some of her views, which naturally changed in some respects over the years in the light of this experience.

In editing her original text of "Spiritualism in the Light of Occult Science" I have confined myself to dividing the chapters into four main parts, which fall logically together, and transferring the one on Clairvoyance from the end of Part One to the beginning of Part Four, where it more appropriately belongs. I have also contributed the titles for the different Parts, but those of the chapters are Dion Fortune's own.

Gareth Knight
All Souls' Day 1998

PART ONE

SPIRITUALISM & OCCULTISM IN PRACTICE

Spiritualism in the Light of Occult Science

In this study of spiritualism it is not proposed to weigh the evidence in regard to the actuality of psychic phenomena; this has been done by such men as Sir William Crookes, Sir Oliver Lodge, and Mr. J.W.Crawford, and their experiments have been repeated so often under test conditions that they may be safely accepted. Fraudulent mediums there will always be as long as there are credulous members of the general public who are willing to put their hands in their pockets. We will not concern ourselves with the sifting of this oft-threshed chaff. Let us accept the facts, as we have reasonable grounds for doing, and proceed forthwith to attempt their elucidation.

Scientific investigators have tried to explain them in terms of psychology; their hypotheses however prove to be no more satisfying than those they would supersede, for psychology itself is in need of a good deal of elucidating, and it may quite well be that psychic science has more to tell us about psychology than psychology has to tell us about psychic science.

There is a school of thought whose opinion has never been asked upon the subject of spiritualism, and it is an opinion which would be well worth having, for the workers in this school are studying closely allied subjects, and their experience throws much light on the findings of psychic research. The occultist is working in the same field as the spiritualist, and as both his motives and theories are different from those of the spiritualist, he comes as an independent witness. In so far as he confirms the spiritualist on the question of fact, his evidence must carry weight, and in so far as he differs from him in the matter of opinion concerning the interpretation to be placed upon the agreed facts, he is also worthy of a hearing, because he may be able to throw light on problems that the spiritualist hypothesis leaves obscure.

Occult science and psychic science approach their natural subject matter from different standpoints. The psychic investigator observes the manifestations of the subtler forms of existence when they have been translated into terms of matter by a medium. Through the intervention of one of those people who have a specialised type of constitution - no more abnormal than the ear of the musician - it is possible to render perceptible to the physical senses things which normally they cannot cognise. It is only when this has been done that the psychic investigator can begin his work. He has to wait for the subtle to impinge upon the dense, observe the effect it has on the dense, and draw his conclusions.

The occultist, on the other hand, by means of the special training of his own mind, enables himself to observe the intangible on its own plane, and does not necessarily bring it through into manifestation in dense matter, though he has in ritual a technique of his own for so doing.

He is, in fact, his own medium. But instead of bringing the intangible through to the plane of matter, he transfers his own consciousness to the subtler planes.

The phenomena which the spiritualist causes to take place are looked upon by the occultist in the same light as the leaping of fish into the air, or the diving of water fowl into a pond. He himself prefers to work on a plane in terms of that plane itself.

With this end in view, he analyses the different forms of existence into their different types; he recognises that, just as there is a faculty of sight which reacts to etheric activity, and a faculty of smell which reacts to gaseous activity, so there are faculties of our minds which react to the different types of existence. They react thus because they are akin to them in nature. We may say, then, that our constitution is not all of a piece, but composite, and that all the different types of existence distinguished by the occultist enter into it.

Four main types of manifestation are recognised - the material, the emotional, the mental, and the spiritual, and each of these types is held to have a denser and a rarer aspect. This fourfold classification represents four entirely different types of manifestation. Each real in every sense of the word; each tangible according to its type; each with its own natural laws; and each interacting with the systems next to it in density, being able to influence that which is more dense but less dynamic than itself, and being influenced by that which is less dense but more dynamic than itself.

For convenience sake, these different planes are arranged schematically in a series, from the densest and the least dynamic to the subtlest and most dynamic. The First Plane is the plane of matter, too well known to need description in these pages. The occultist, for his own convenience, divides it into the Dense and the Etheric Sub-planes. The Dense Sub-plane consists of matter in its solid, liquid, and gaseous states; the Etheric is known to us through the activities of magnetism, light, heat, certain aspects of sound, all radio-activity, and certain other less known forms of force which have long been known to the yogi and the juju man but have not yet been discovered by science, although it is beginning to draw very near to them, and it is probably only a matter of time until the discovery is made. Such systems as homeopathy, such instruments as the emanometer are opening up this plane.

Primitive man believed that every object had a soul. The modern physicist knows that every object has a magnetic field. It is really two different ways of saying the same thing. Every atom of matter is an electric circuit with its consequent magnetic field. Upon this the physicist and occultist are agreed. But, says the occultist, there is known to me what I call a Prime Atom in relation to each plane. That is to say, a unit which forms the root-substance out of which a plane of existence is developed, and it belongs, not to that plane itself, but to the plane above, relatively less dense, relatively more dynamic. This fact is the key to the whole problem. An atom, according to the use made of the term in occult science, is a portion of the substance of a plane which, for the purposes of that plane, behaves as a unit and is indivisible. But, viewed from the standpoint of the plane above, it is a molecule, being an association of atoms of that plane. The atoms of dense matter are, nevertheless, composed of associations of electrons; they are, therefore, composite when viewed from the standpoint of the Etheric Plane. The Prime Atom or the fundamental unit of the Etheric Plane is the electron, but the electron, when viewed from the standpoint of what the occultist calls the Astral Plane, is composite in its turn.

The Astral Plane may be defined as the plane of life force, of vitality; and life, considered apart from the vehicles through which it manifests itself is *emotion*. We see it in the great fundamental instincts and the accompanying passions. We see it sublimated into the tender affections related to ideas. In order to realise this concept we need a form of thought which will enable us to conceive the change-over from matter to consciousness which takes place on the etheric-astral borderline. It is this which occult science endeavours to supply by means of its symbol systems. It is those symbol systems, which, taken literally by inadequately instructed students as well as by the uninitiated, are the cause of much misunderstanding and confusion, and lead to the accusation of self deception and superstition being levelled at the Ancient Wisdom. As a matter of fact, these symbol systems are really an algebra which enables us to compute the intangible.

Occult science, then, teaches that every object has an etheric counterpart, and natural sciences, though using other terms, would agree. Occult science would go farther than this, and say that many objects have a vital aspect, an organised system of life forces in addition to their etheric system. Natural science, though perhaps not prepared to commit itself to this statement, in the absence of evidence of a nature that it can accept, would nevertheless hardly be prepared to deny it. Occult science goes on yet further, and says that in many of the types of existence that have physical, etheric, and vital organised systems, there is also an organised system of ideas or mind. Natural science would, we presume, concede this also.

Here, however, comes the point where occult science parts company with natural science. It does not hold that life begins with simple forms of matter, but with simple forms of consciousness. It carries to its logical conclusions the dictum that it is not form which creates function, but function which creates form. The life preceded the form in which it manifested itself. It is not, according to the occult hypothesis, the physical form which gives rise to its etheric counterpart of electromagnetic stresses, but the etheric counterpart, organised by life-forces which in their turn are organised by consciousness, which holds the molecules composing the physical body as in a network, wherein each article rests in its appointed etheric socket.

It is possible to conceive, therefore, that were all the material particles withdrawn, there would still remain an etheric framework. It is this etheric framework, organised and capable of responding to the directing influence of consciousness, which is the basis of all supernormal phenomena which involve manifestations on the material plane - raps, levitations, apports, the touch of ghostly hands - all these are due to the properties of the etheric sub-plane of matter - the aspect of matter which can be controlled by mind.

It is well known among occultists that the etheric counterpart of the arm or leg can be withdrawn from its physical form and used independently. It is done by thinking of the limb as being in a different position to that which it actually occupies. When this is done with sufficient concentration, the kinaesthetic sense, which automatically tells us the position the body occupies, disappears from the limb; and as the sense of position is noted subjectively to have disappeared, a psychic, observing the experiment, would tell us that the etheric limb was seen to be coming out as a shadowy ghost limb which, under certain conditions of light, may even be visible to ordinary sight. It is this phenomenon which produces the well known hysterical symptom of glove and stocking anaesthesia and hysterical paralysis. Emotional shock or tension causes the extrusion of the etheric counterpart of the limb by concentratedly wishing it were in some different position from the one it actually occupies. It is a common experience for an occultist after a projection experiment to be uncoordinated in his movements for a few minutes, owing to the etheric counterpart not being at once fully reabsorbed.

People vary greatly in their power to extrude an etheric limb; some can do it readily, others only in a minor degree and with great effort. Experience shows, however, that everybody parts with a certain amount of etheric substance fairly readily, though not always in an organised form. A materialising medium is a person who can extrude large amounts of it in that unorganised form which is called ectoplasm.

This type of matter appears to be readily moulded by the mind. Herein we may find the clue to the many curious effects produced by the mind on the body. The effects of repercussion, the stigmata of the saints, the injuries to an unborn child inflicted by the emotion of its mother - all these are ectoplasmic phenomena.

If organised consciousness survives bodily death it is easy to conceive of it moulding this ectoplasm into a body for manifestation if it desires sufficiently ardently to manifest and were able to draw to itself sufficient ectoplasm for the purpose.

How much of the physical phenomena which occur at a séance are due to the projection of the etheric limbs of the medium, and how much are due to the use of unorganised ectoplasm by a disembodied entity, is a matter which has to be ascertained in each individual case. The occultist would unhesitatingly aver that all psychic phenomena cannot be ascribed to disembodied entities, though he would not exclude their intervention; but he knows that he himself can produce many supernatural phenomena at will by projecting an etheric limb, or even the etheric body itself as a whole.

It is a usual experience to feel a cold wind sweep round a circle just before a spirit manifestation is about to commence. Occultists believe that this sensation is due to a small amount of etheric substance being withdrawn from the sitters in that circle. As good materialising mediums are rare, occultists are accustomed to use other substances than human ectoplasm for the purposes of enabling entities to materialise. The emanations of freshly shed blood serve equally well; and it was for this reason that blood sacrifices were employed in certain cults. Certain aromatic substances, when burnt, give off an etheric emanation which, although it will not produce as tangible a manifestation as the vital fluids, will nevertheless enable a fairly solid form to be fabricated. The grave objections attendant upon the use of blood for materialising purposes cause it never to be used by reputable occultists; but in black magic, where the experiments are carried out regardless of the moral consequences, it is not infrequently employed.

It is a curious fact that, in ritual magic, where incense is used as the basis of manifestation, instead of the usual sensation of coldness experienced by the participants in psychic experiments, the temperature rises most markedly. Anyone who is used to experimenting in ritual magic knows that he must start in a cool room, or the atmosphere will be unbearable before he has finished.

This is attributed to the fact that instead of vitality being withdrawn from the sitters in the circle for the purposes of the experiment, vitality is being poured in by the invisible participants.

Out of the principles enumerated in the foregoing pages, it will be found possible to construct a working theory of spirit manifestation, based on the properties of the etheric form of matter, a form which is capable of being manipulated by mind.

All these different types of supernormal phenomena are produced by the same means. The occultist, able to produce them at will, can tell us a very great deal about them, because he knows how he goes to work when he intends to produce them. He knows that by means of concentrated thought he can manipulate this subtle aspect of matter, akin to electricity. He concludes that it is by similar means that similar results are produced by others, whether that other be a pregnant woman, a saint, or a disembodied spirit.

Communication with the Departed

There are two questions which are frequently asked. Firstly, why is it that the spirits who communicate with the spiritualist deny reincarnation, or at least have no knowledge of it, and the spirits to whom the occultist looks for his instruction take it for granted? And secondly, why is it that the occultist discountenances attempts to communicate with the departed?

In order to answer these questions explanation of the occultist's theories concerning death must be given; for in the light of these theories the answer to both these questions can be seen.

Death, according to the occultist, commences when the soul withdraws from the physical body, but does not finish then. The process of death goes through certain stages, each of which might be called a death in itself.

The human organisation is composed of several different, distinct, but co-operating systems, and when disintegration occurs, these separate one from another and are resolved into their elements; there is, however, an interregnum of varying length between the separation of the organised systems one from another and their final resolution into their elements when "the body returns to the dust and the spirit to God that gave it."

When the first stage of death occurs, the soul, that is to say, the composite consciousness of the personality, withdraws from the physical body. The physical body consists of two distinct organised systems, the body of dense matter, solid, liquid, and gaseous, and the system of electromagnetic stresses of which natural science is beginning to be aware and which occult science has long known and used. Consciousness withdraws from both these systems simultaneously, and for a brief period they remain together. Then the etheric death takes place, and the etheric counterpart withdraws from the dense physical body, which thereupon rapidly succumbs to the onslaughts of the disintegrating influences which only the forces of vitality have enabled it to keep at bay. The saprophytic bacteria fulfil their function as scavengers, and the body is reduced to its elements which then become available once again for the purposes of life.

The system of magnetic stresses which is known to us as the etheric double does not immediately disintegrate; three days normally elapse from the moment of departure of the soul to the commencement of disintegration of the etheric body. It is for this reason that occultists advise that cremation should be delayed till three days after the physical death. There are certain abnormal conditions, however, in which the etheric double holds together much longer than the normal period. The occultist considers that such a prolongation of a transition state is pathological and highly undesirable, for it means that a soul is still attached to the etheric counterpart. The words, "a soul" are used advisedly, for it need not necessarily be the original soul which is thus attached. The etheric counterpart is like a discarded garment - anyone can put it on.

It may well be asked why any disembodied spirit should desire to maintain itself on the frontiers of death by clinging to an etheric counterpart which normally should be disintegrating. The motive in most cases is fear. As soon as the soul is freed from its material body, both physical and etheric, it goes to the Judgement Hall of Osiris, in the picturesque phrase of the ancient initiates; or, in the psychological terminology of the modern occultist, it faces its realisation. All the incidents of its past life pass in review before it and it is compelled to assess them. Evidence in support of this statement may be found in the fact that people who are revived after apparent death by drowning frequently report this experience. Their past life rises up before their eyes, they tell us, after the initial struggles cease. It is this subjective realisation which constitutes both the heaven and hell so vividly delineated by theology.

It is not surprising that the soul with a bad record, confronted by the vision of its own life, refuses to face its memories, and does in death what the neurotic does in life - dissociates. Attention cannot be forced; what it will not look at it does not see, and what it does not see it cannot abreact, and so the winding-up of the affairs of the previous life is held up.

Such a suspension of the normal processes of disincarnation also occurs when there is an intense fear of death or an intense desire to cling to life. The breakdown of the physical machinery forces the soul out of the dense body, but it clings desperately to the etheric counterpart. Now this etheric counterpart is built by the mind, not by the body; it is not the disintegration of the body that causes its break-up, but the withdrawal of the organised forces of consciousness, and it is the break-up of the etheric counterpart which permits the disintegration of the physical body to take place. As long as vitality is present, it will hold decomposition at bay; when it is withdrawn, necrosis takes place, whether of a tissue or the entire organism.

The third cause which leads to the ensouling of an etheric counterpart is the deliberate action of an occultist who, possessing the necessary knowledge, determines on this psychic crime. For reasons best known to himself he does not wish to face the Judgement Hall of Osiris, and he employs this device to maintain himself in the transition stage of life in death.

The length of time for which this condition may be maintained depends upon circumstances. The etheric counterpart is really an electric storage battery. The physical body is the dynamo which generates the electricity with which it is charged; if it were possible completely to insulate the etheric counterpart, it would continue to exist indefinitely but in actual practice this is not possible. The electrical energy slowly diffuses away and unless it is recharged the etheric counterpart disintegrates. When it is being held together by a soul, however, a certain amount of recharging takes place, and it is this that constitutes the danger of the earth-bound to the living - emotional rapport brings the "ghost" into touch with both its friends and its enemies on the physical plane, and from their bodies it is able to recharge its own etheric form to a certain extent. This accounts for the extreme exhaustion which suddenly supervenes in those who have been in close emotional relationship with the dying; a collapse which is not accounted for by physical exhaustion. For the impersonal hospital nurse who may have borne the heaviest end of the burden is unaffected by it.

This is a process which normally goes on at death; to allow it to take place is an act of mercy to the departing soul, for it gives it a sense of security and comfort as it first comes out into the unfamiliar conditions of the Unseen World. It is for this reason that people crave for the presence of their loved ones round their death bed, and those who love them are able to given them this comfort and help as they pass out, provided they are prepared to endure the temporary discomfort. It is when the normal act of psychic charity is overdone that it becomes pathological and injurious to both giver and receiver.

It is in order to supply this magnetic element to the departed soul and save it from the shock of sudden disintegration that candles are kept burning beside a corpse, and fresh flowers laid upon it, for these both supply a form of magnetic energy, which, though less potent than human vitality, nevertheless is better than nothing, and serves to tide the soul over the first shock of transition; for remember, the sufferings of death do not end with the moment of physical death, and our care and service should follow our beloved some distance into the future life.

It is interesting to note that it was to delay the leakage of energy from the etheric double, in order to give the soul as long as possible between incarnations, that the Egyptians embalmed their dead; while the Hindus, another race with natural occult aptitude, burn their dead in order to ensure the release of the soul and its departure to its own place. Our own system of earth burial is as good as can be found in normal cases, for it permits of the processes of death to proceed unhurried, and where occult science is but little understood, cases of necromancy are sufficiently rare to require no special precautions to be taken against them in the ordinary way; but where there is any reason to suspect obsession, it is far wiser to resort to cremation, for that dispatches the soul to its own place whether it likes it or not, destroying its *point d'appui* before it has time to construct for itself another.

When all these facts, well known to esoteric science, are taken into consideration, it will be seen why occultists object to the practice of trying to get in touch with the dead through mediums, thereby recalling their attention to the life they have just left. To send out thoughts after to help them on their journey is one thing, and is considered by the occultist to be not only an act of mercy but an important duty; but to recall the departed to our sphere is to do them an injury, and occultists deplore the prevalence of the practice. The departed have no need to communicate with the living, save in rare cases when some duty has been left undischarged, and it is far better and more humane that the living gain their certainty of a future life from the philosophical considerations of occult science than by vivisection of the departed, however well-intentioned.

Spirit-teaching and Reincarnation

Why is it that the spirits who communicate with occultists teach reincarnation and the spirits who communicate with spiritualists deny it? This is a question which is often asked. It might appear at first sight that this direct contradiction of testimony must throw doubt on the whole question of life after death. A closer examination of the matter will reveal, however, that this is not so. The communicating entities are speaking in the light of two different types of experience, and their contradictory statements are what would be expected. Far from denying the occult hypothesis, the statements made by spirit communicators bear it out. This may appear paradoxical, but an understanding of the esoteric doctrines concerning post-mortem conditions will reveal the solution of the problem.

After the soul has finally severed its connection with the body, which, as we have seen in the previous chapter, does not occur with the passing of the breath, but when the etheric death takes place three days later, it enters upon the second phase of its discarnate existence. Its consciousness is that of its prime, for it retains all it acquired during its last incarnation and is no longer hampered in the use of its faculties by worn out bodily organs.

Its organism now consists of:

(1) the spark of Divine Spirit which is the nucleus of all human existence;
(2) the spiritual nature, consisting of spiritual qualities;
(3) the power of abstract thought, or Higher Mind;
(4) the power of concrete thought, or Lower Mind; and
(5) the emotional nature.

Each of these is a thing in itself, an organised system of reacting forces. Each normally functions in co-operation with all the others, but is capable, under certain conditions, of independent function. It will be seen that two other organised systems of forces go to the making of the complete man, the physical and the etheric; these, however, have already gone into the discard, and the Ego is left with its subtler aspects only. We have, therefore, a complete human consciousness, unchanged by death, but minus a physical body. It lacks sense organs by means of which to contact the plane of dense matter, and its subtler sense organs have been released for function by the casting off of the physical body, therefore the plane of its consciousness is changed. It has ceased to be aware of what is happening on the earth plane, but it is still aware of the feelings of those with whom it is in emotional rapport.

For a varying period it exists on this plane, pulling itself together and making its adjustments to its new phase of existence, it still has full memory of its past life, and its interests only gradually detach themselves from the things of that life. It is still, as it were, looking back over its shoulder. Gradually, however, it is being weaned from its old ties. Memories fade, new interests are awakened; consciousness is making its adaptation.

The plane on which the soul now finds itself is called, in esoteric terminology, the "Antechamber of Osiris." It is not a place, however, (there are no places in the geographical sense upon the subtler planes) but is a state of consciousness - a state of consciousness, however, which the soul possesses in common with all other souls that share in it; the limitation of the physical body, which keeps consciousness separate, being gone.

It is while in this state that the soul is most readily contacted by those who would link the living with the dead. It is the Antechamber of Osiris which is spirit life as known to the spiritualist. Here souls live among their own thought forms, the creations of their own imagination; each in a subjective world of his own, yet able to perceive the subjective worlds of others because the barriers of brain consciousness are down. Here live and work those beings whose task it is to rule and supervise the souls waiting in the Antechamber, to attend to their needs and assist them to adjust to their new conditions.

It is of the conditions in the Antechamber that the souls of the departed tell those they leave behind them when a medium acts as telephone. The entities who live and work on this plane never tell what they know concerning that which lies beyond the barrier because it is forbidden them to do so. The Antechamber of Osiris is like a lock on a river; there must be no leakage from up-stream till the down-stream gates are shut. In due course, however, it is observed that the souls of the departed tell those who are keeping in touch with them that they have received a summons to go on, and will no longer be able to communicate as they did heretofore. It may be that messages will be received from them through spirit friends on the inner planes, but the actual voice of the departed is heard no more for a time. The summons has come to the Judgement Hall of Osiris.

In other words, the soul having made its adjustment to its new stage of consciousness, sinks into a state of profound meditation on the events of its past life. It sees them in their true significance and experiences as much regret as it is capable of feeling, thereby abreacting them. This is Purgatory. For the hardened soul that will not feel regret there is also Hell, wherein the consequences of its own evil nature react upon it. The soul who sincerely desires to amend does not experience Hell; that is reserved for the unrepentant sinner who remains there until it is borne in upon him that evil had better be avoided.

After the period of repentance and realisation has been passed through, the tenor of consciousness begins to change; the soul, still in a subjective state but having worked out its emotional reactions to the past, now begins to work upon it intellectually according to its capacity, realising the spiritual significance of the events of its past life. Its mood has changed. Its emotional reactions towards the past have been worked out; it has no more acute emotion left, but only those generalised regrets and desires that determine temperament in the next incarnation. Its passions are burnt out. Its emotional consciousness has also gone into the discard, even as did its physical body. Death has progressed another stage.

The discarnated soul now consists of an intellect overshadowed by a spiritual nature. Memory of the past life still remains, but the attitude of the soul towards it is impersonal; it seeks to understand; it has ceased to feel. Souls remain in this state for varying periods according to the amount of mental development they possess. In souls of very rudimentary intellect, objective consciousness is not achieved on this plane, and they remain in a subconscious state as in sleep.

When all the meditation concerning its past life of which that soul is capable has been performed, the Second Death occurs. Even the memories of the past life then go into the discard. The personality is dead, finished. But what survives? The abstract mind and spiritual nature survive, forming what in occult terminology is called the Individuality. It is this alone which is immortal. The Personality is as mortal as the body. This does not mean, however, that the individualised existence ends with the Second Death. It is immortal and eternal, never born and undying. Only its objective consciousness is withdrawn stage by stage at each successive death taking with it the absorbed essence of the experiences of incarnated existence. That is to say, the Individuality, or higher self, realises the spiritual significance of these experiences of an incarnation and profits by them, and that is all it needs to know. The abstract mind retains the abstract essence of all the past lives, just as a phial of digitalis contains the abstract essence of a spinney of foxgloves.

We are now in a position to distinguish between the Personality, which is the unit of incarnation, and the Individuality, which is the unit of evolution - a distinction of the utmost importance in occult science. It is in the light of this distinction that all considerations concerning communications with the departed must apply.

The occultist considers that the processes of disincarnation continue long after the death of the physical body, and he deprecates any interference with these processes as being detrimental to the interests of the departed spirit. We should give our dead their quittance and allow them to go on freely to their own place, confining our activities on their behalf to sending loving thoughts to cheer and companion them on their journey. We should no more seek to hold them back than a mother should seek to prevent her son from leaving home to go out into the world when his time has come. To summon the dead to come back and comfort the living, which is all it really amounts to, is an act of selfishness, just as much as is the misguided love of a mother who calls a son away from his work to keep her company at the fireside. She is wasting his time and spoiling his opportunities. It is no more fair to a departed soul to recall it to the earth life than it is fair to a youth to keep him tied to apron strings. It is for this reason that the occultist disapproves of the spiritualist's activities in connection with communication with the dead.

Communication with a soul that is passing through the different stages of death is one thing, and communication with a dweller in the spirit world is another. Souls who have learnt all that the earth life can teach them no longer need to incarnate, but continue their evolution on the subtler planes. And not only do they grow and evolve thereon themselves, but they also have their work to do; they have passed beyond the stage when they float like animalcule in the current of evolution, they are self conscious, self directing entities, intelligently co-operating with the work of God. To come into touch with these is a very different matter from disturbing the dead.

To contact them, however, it is necessary to rise to a much higher level of consciousness than to contact the souls of the departed who have not yet passed the Gates of Osiris. Only very highly developed mediums can make the contact; they are beyond the reach of the average psychic.

There are two types of discarnate souls then whom the medium can contact - the souls that are living and working upon the subtle planes, and souls who are only sojourning there between incarnations. We have shown in detail the processes by which the discarnating of a soul goes on. It will be seen, therefore, that if communication is established before the soul has cast off the last of the limitations of the lower self, it will still be viewing things from the standpoint of the incarnation just finished. If, however, a soul be contacted which is no longer bound to the wheel of birth and death, as the old Eastern phrase expresses it, that soul will view things from the standpoint of the immortal spirit, eternal, unborn, undying, evolving with the evolution of the solar system. It is these perfected souls alone with which the occultist seeks to establish communication.

The consciousness of the Personality is built up in the brief span between birth and death; as long as we are communicating with that consciousness we shall hear nothing concerning reincarnation because *the Personality does not reincarnate*, its essence being absorbed by the Higher Self at the end of each incarnation. It is only when we touch the levels of consciousness which compose the Individuality that we shall receive teaching concerning reincarnation, for it is only the Higher Self which survives bodily death. The

Personality, being built up during the life of the body, does not remember its predecessors in the long line of the evolution of the immortal spirit that ensouls it. It has no knowledge of the Second Death until it experiences it, and then it cannot communicate through the average medium who offers his services. Up to a certain stage of spiritual unfolding, the soul is driven in blinkers by the Lords of Humanity or Racial Angels, as they are sometimes called. Its vision is limited to the task in hand lest it should be confused by a multiplicity of experience which it has no means of sorting or assimilating. To ask such a one concerning cosmic things is a waste of time. He may answer according to his lights, but his lights are dim. The trained occultist spends no time with such communicators unless circumstances should cause him to lend them a helping hand. He himself, being an initiate and therefore able to function with the consciousness of the Higher Self, knows a great deal more about the Inner Planes than they do, and is in a position to give help rather than to receive it.

In view of all this, it may be asked why it was that the spiritualistic movement was ever started, or that spirits can be found willing to co-operate with it? The answer to this question involves a further explanation of the nature of the unseen side of life as understood by the occultist.

Evolution reached the lowest point of its descent into matter during the nineteenth century. At that point there is great danger of an evolution sticking at a dead centre; the centrifugal impulse has spent its force and the attraction of the centre has not yet made itself felt. The tide is neither ebbing nor flowing, but at slack water. It is exactly comparable to the process which is gone through when an engine is reversed. It has to be stopped before it can be re-started, even if that stoppage be of the briefest.

Some means had to be found to re-start the wheels of evolution in their reversed movement, for whereas they had hitherto been descending into matter, they now had to turn round and ascend back to spirit. Something had to be done to induce men to change their view-point, and whatever was done had to be drastic, for not otherwise could the attention of the crowd be caught and held.

The spiritualist movement was started by the spirits themselves for this purpose. A number of them undertook to produce phenomena which should startle humanity into a new concept. They got out of the train of evolution in which they had been travelling, put their shoulders to the wheel, and heaved it off its dead centre. The story of that undertaking can be read in the history of the early days of spiritualism.

Communication with the departed ought to be taken as an established fact at the present day, and we should no longer disturb our dead by hallooing after them with the help of a medium. It is too near akin to the trick of the small boy who shouted after the man in a hurry until he returned to enquire what was wanted of him, only to be asked, "How far would you have got by now if I hadn't called you back?" There is much work still to be done in psychic research, and the great entities concerned with the spiritualist movement are engaged in it, and are giving us some very wonderful results, especially in the work concerning ectoplasm. But there is far too much playing about with the subtler planes. It is unwholesome for both communicator and sitter, and has developed a class of spirits only one degree from the earth-bound entities we considered in a previous chapter. These spirits are able to maintain themselves in the Antechamber of Osiris and do not take their call to go on to the judgement. They are not necessarily evil in any way, but their development is arrested. It is this cloud of ignorant witnesses which is obscuring the issues for the spiritualist movement at the present moment. They are expert at communicating and come through easily, therefore they are much in evidence at séances, especially public ones, to which the higher types of spirit will not come.

Those entities whom occultists call the Masters only communicate with those who have been trained in their own tradition. An initiate of an occult tradition has access to the Masters connected with that tradition, and until he is of a high degree, is advised to refuse contact with all others. The trained occultist takes great precautions to ensure that he shall only be in touch with reliable entities; he considers that the average medium does not take anything like sufficient precautions, and consequently gets unsatisfactory communications. It is like a modern hospital nurse, thoroughly drilled in asepsis, watching the surgical methods of Sairey Gamp. A heated argument is apt to arise. The hospital nurse objects to the risks, and Sairy Gamp objects to the trouble. I do not mean by these words to impugn the work of high class mediums who lend themselves to the experimentation of qualified observers; such work is done under conditions which the occultist would agree are satisfactory, but there are, unfortunately, a great many Sairey Gamps in the psychic world, with their advertisements in its various periodicals, and the spiritual sepsis which claims so many victims is not infrequently due to the psychic infection of their dirty hands. It is high time there were some check on the tendency to run to psychics without adequate motive or enquiry; the people who do so contribute no more to psychic science than the people who go up in an aeroplane for ten minutes at a fête contribute to the science of aeronautics; and it is a further drawback to the promiscuous séance-sitters that they encourage the worst element in spiritualism - the element that brings it into disrepute.

There is a great work to be done in the field of psychic research; the spiritualist is steadily and patiently proving his case upon scientific principles. The occultist knows many things which he has never attempted to prove to the satisfaction of inductive science. The advance of psychic science is bringing these facts within the range of laboratory experiment. The occultist ought to place his data at the disposal of the psychic research worker so that it may be reduced to a form in which it can no longer be either denied or ignored.

COMMENTARY
Gareth Knight

It was not long after founding The Society of the Inner Light that Dion Fortune wrote her two books on spiritualism, initially as series of articles in her group's magazine "The Inner Light".

The first, "Spiritualism in the Light of Occult Science," which is reproduced as the main text of the present volume, appeared between January 1929 and April 1930, and was immediately followed between May 1930 and April 1931 by "Through the Gates of Death".

The latter title was intended to be a practical source of comfort and self-help for members of the lay public when confronted with bereavement. The earlier text is a more specialist look at the different methods and assumptions of spiritualism from the point of view and experience of the occultist.

Comments in both works upset some spiritualists. Perhaps not surprisingly, when she advises against trying to make contact with the recently departed.

She was not decrying spiritualism root and branch, but felt it her duty to point out that before we attempt such communication, particularly when in the emotional intensity of immediate personal grief, we should carefully consider our motives, and the possible effect we might be having upon those we are calling back. The dead may have their emotional problems as well as the living.

There are, for example, unhealthy emotional dependencies in life in the world and it helps nobody if we attempt to extend these beyond the grave. There is more than one kind of love, and some kinds that are none too healthy; such as a possessive demand for affection, care and attention, rather than real concern for the interests and well being of the beloved. At its worst this can be a subtle form of vampirism, the deceased being persistently called back to continue to provide the emotional support given during physical life.

At a slightly higher level are those who seek to relieve an inner emotional tension by pouring demonstrative affection and service upon the loved one, irrespective of the latter's needs in the matter. It could be equally reprehensible to try to continue this kind of suffocating possessiveness beyond the grave.

In short, Dion Fortune did not so much decry all attempts at communication with the departed but pointed out that it should only be done for very good reason.

It followed from this that members of her Society at the time were not encouraged to attend spiritualist meetings. This led to considerable heart searching amongst some members, and to the resignation of at least one, W.E.Butler, who later achieved prominence as a respected writer on occult topics and much loved teacher in his own right.

All this was in the early 1930's, but by the time the 2nd World War had got under way, with a resumption of the carnage that had brought about a renewal of spiritualism during and after the 1st World War, Dion Fortune felt impelled to modify her views.

This apparently was the result of a deliberate push from her own inner plane sources, and it would appear that it was felt in those circles that a unique opportunity was presented. This was to try to bring together the separate movements of occultism and spiritualism with a view to a great resurgence of inner awareness in the post-war years.

With the benefit of hindsight it may seem that this initiative was somewhat premature, and that any real breaking down of the bastions of materialism would have to wait until the 1960's and the various manifestations of what later became known as the New Age movement. For their part, students of occultism and spiritualism still seem to be content to live in their separate houses and keep their own company. In 1941/2 however, all seemed ready to play for, and the particular initiative in which Dion Fortune played a prominent part makes for fascinating reading.

It begins with a change of editorial chair in a spiritualist newspaper of the time known as "Light". Charles Cammell was appointed editor in September 1941, and later said, in an editorial of February 1942, that he felt he had been placed there by higher powers to undertake a specific task. In support of this he recalled a sequence of significant events that led to his appointment, which were later confirmed by various psychic communications.

These included a vivid dream. In this dream he met a person whose identity he recognised, even though he had never seen her before "in life or in portrait". Some months later he was invited to attend a séance held by a small and strictly limited circle of students, and it was here, in the role of the medium, that he met the person he had seen in his dream. It was of course Dion Fortune.

It so happens that we have a transcript of this particular meeting, which occurred on 27th October 1941 and was on the subject of conditions required for good trance mediumship and the modus operandi of trance communications. Both subjects of course, close to Charles Cammell's heart.

Desirable conditions for Trance Mediumship

It is desirable to have a room small rather than large in order to concentrate the atmosphere.

The larger the room the more power is necessary in order to make a suitable atmosphere.

If a large room is used it would be desirable to have a canopy and a curtain around the couch of the medium.

The couch should be flat and firm so that the head and spine of the medium are in a straight line, head slightly raised. (You generally make the mistake of having the medium's head too high.)

The temperature should be even, with no draughts and the light as dim as possible. It is not easy for the communicating entity to come into possession of the medium if the light in the room is bright. The medium will seldom work well in an unfamiliar room.

Once the trance is well established it is not readily disturbed. A sudden, sharp noise, or sudden bright light will disturb it. But while the medium is going into trance any small or fidgety noise is liable to prevent her from going off.

When the sitters are gathered together, there should be a short space of time before trance to enable them to settle down and concentrate their minds on the topic of the trance.

If the trance is one of a series, they would do well to discuss or read aloud from the previous communication.

If a new sitter is being introduced (and only one at a time should be introduced if possible,) it is a good plan to discuss the matter of trance in general, for the minds of those forming the circle play an important part in the bringing through of communications.

When the communicating entity speaks, each person should answer, thus establishing contact.

Persons asking questions should speak softly as a loud voice disturbs the medium.

There should be no discussion between members of the circle, but only between individuals and the communicator, or the trance will be disturbed.

If it is desired to make some rearrangement of the room, or any person wishes to withdraw, they should treat the communicator as if he were the chairman of a meeting and ask his permission to do what is desired. This will not interfere with trance if all movements are quiet and, especially, *unhurried*.

It is desirable, when trance is prolonged, that precautions be taken against undue fatigue on the part of the scribe or any of the sitters. There is no reason why you should not change scribes in the course of a communication.

When the trance is concluded, the sitters should wait quietly, without talking, till the medium recovers consciousness, because during that period she may be communicating herself with the communicator. Moreover, she has to establish conscious control of her own subconsciousness again.

Modus operandi of trance communications

It is quite simple if you understand the rationale of hypnosis. The medium, by first relaxing completely and then concentrating on the image of the communicator, disconnects the conscious mind from the subconsciousness. This is done by gathering the focus of attention to a single point, and holding it there until the mind ceases to register. This disconnects the levels of consciousness. The point on which attention is concentrated is the *image* of the communicator.

Consequently, when the directing mind is disconnected, as it were, the subconsciousness has this image imprinted on it.

The communicating entity, who is a mind without a body, visualises his own image, and the two images being identical, a telepathic rapport with the medium's subconsciousness is established.

The subconscious mind of the medium then dramatises the personality of the control. The control conveys ideas to the subconscious mind of the medium telepathically. These ideas are archetypal or abstract. That is why it is so difficult to convey names or numbers. It is the dramatised, artificial personality created by the mind of the medium which talks to you. If there is within the scope of the medium's knowledge, the material out of which the trance address can be made, it is utilised. If the material is lacking, a symbolic method of presentation has to be used.

Persons who are naturally of mediumistic type are quite different from the trained medium used by a Mystery School. Natural or spontaneous mediumship is a pathological trait, and bordering upon mental disease.

The trained medium is taught how to dissociate the levels of a well-knit mind, and how to take the initial steps in the dramatisation of the personality of the communicator. These acts are voluntary, whereas in the natural medium they are involuntary; and that person is only saved from the consequences of dissociation of personality and the dramatisation of the secondary personality by the intervention of a spirit guide. In the absence of a spirit guide the dissociation of the personality and development of secondary personalities follow the ordinary course of a psychopathic manifestation. It frequently happens that a medium of this type who has worked well under a spirit guide may lose contact with that guide and then become merely a schizophrenic. Or the guide may sometimes be in touch with the medium, sometimes not, and so the quality of the trance will vary.

Trance communications should always be judged by their intrinsic content, because once the image has been built, the subconscious mind of the medium can produce a perfectly good simulacrum of the communicator.

In the light of this explanation you will see why it is that a medium of an unevolved type of personality has for control a child or a savage, for the limitations of the medium's personality are such that these are adequate presentations. Such persons, being themselves children at heart, the communicator is limited by the nature of the medium, save in the matter of symbolic presentations, of which the prophets of the Old Testament afford an example.

The question of language presents no real difficulty, because the ideas are formulated by the control in terms of the higher mind which has an abstract type of mentation.

The translation into concrete concepts takes place in the medium's subconsciousness. Terms or names with which the medium is unfamiliar have either to be spelt out by the communicator or communicated phonetically.

The personality of the Communicator, however, if well

dramatised, should come through very clearly and be able to establish direct telepathic contact with the minds of the sitters. This contact plays a very important part in their development.

Séance Transcript of November 26th 1941

This meeting was followed up by another, between 5.40 and 7.40 p.m. on November 26th 1941, when the ideas and general plan of campaign were spelled out by Dion Fortune's inner communicator. The gist of this trance address was again the subject of a later Editorial by Charles Cammell, who observed some of the strictures of the communicator, in particular that "The teaching must be published as from an unknown communicator through an unknown medium. The communications must be judged on their intrinsic value."

Cammell also omitted some of the more confidential remarks and instructions in his later editorial. We give, however, the full text of the original meeting. In this N stands for the communicator, C for C.R.Cammell.

N: A man who dies a fool or a knave continues to be so; the same applies to a sensible man, except that he is less well informed about matters on the physical plane but better informed about matters on his own plane.

You, Cammell, have two gods; you are sincerely dedicated to the pursuit of truth and beauty.

Why have you been permitted to contact me? You are in a key position and hold the means of publicity. You will meet difficulties; if you are not careful and diplomatic you may be dislodged. You must make haste slowly.

There is a piece of work to be done and for that I can promise you my support and assistance. I can tell the set of the invisible currents.

The Spiritualist Movement may be said to have arisen in the third quarter of the last century; it achieved importance and influence during the last war.

There has always been a tradition of the Secret Wisdom. It has been in the hands of specially trained and suitable persons; they have had knowledge and power beyond the average. They have always been a spiritual and intellectual élite and, in some ages, a political élite.

That tradition has never been broken. It has had its great and its decadent periods. It has fallen into decadence because humanity, most unfortunately, is human. One such period was due to the scepticism of the so-called Age of Reason.

In the third quarter of the last century there arose a new impulse. This impulse came through certain women: the first ripples of the Aquarian tide. There were several movements which utilised and developed higher modes of consciousness, e.g. Spiritualism, Theosophy and Christian Science.

All the time the Ancient Tradition was in the background.

The deeper teachings are reserved for the few. It is not a question of secrecy for its own sake, but for the same reason that only a few can be taught Higher Mathematics.

The war of 1914-1918 marked the end of the Piscean Age. And during that war and the epidemic that followed, millions of souls passed over, and the gates had to be opened widely.

There are certain souls, freed from the wheel of birth and death, who, foregoing their rest, elect to serve in the Earth atmosphere. They are organised among themselves according to the type of technique used in life; also those of the same races and cultures are organised by mutual sympathy.

These beings send messages to humanity. They released to humanity knowledge of the immortality of the soul during the war and epidemic; otherwise the shadow would have been too dark to endure. Hence the growth of the Spiritualist Movement; the gulf was bridged.

Now I come to where my work begins and possibly yours.

This war sees us coming out of the reign of chaos. In the last war humanity descended into the valley; during this war, with infinite labour, it is climbing out, and there is coming a new phase of enlightenment. Spiritualism during the last war; esoteric knowledge is being given out in this; you will have noticed the evidence about you everywhere. The pioneering aspect of Spiritualism has passed.

[There came an explanation, not recorded in the transcript, of how Cammell, allegedly holding very loosely to Spiritualism, was put into a key position.]

C: Your counsel will be of enormous value.

N: The ordinary spiritualist will reject intellectual pabulum only. His attitude is a religious one; you may say that communication is his god. But remember the pioneers are not to be despised; they are entitled to their reward. But the position is this: they reject human reason and accept anything from the inner planes.

The scientific psychical researchers have been driving a tunnel from their side; those on the Other Side have been doing the same; the two tunnels will meet if the calculations are true.

Part of our work is the reconciliation of first principles with scientific findings. We have to make available to the psychical researchers the knowledge of the Esoteric Tradition.

Those who learn to rise up the planes during life can descend down the planes after death. But only those of the same technique and tradition communicate.

The technique is the same as that of Spiritualism but there is a difference in the calibre of the communicator. It is not in my province to produce phenomena.

It is a question of co-ordinating activities and giving out teaching for the new age.

I can tell you what has already happened on my plane and *will* work out on yours.

There can only be a partial presentation of teaching because it is limited by the receptive capacity of the reader or listener.

There will be a modicum of teaching as to the practical impact of the teaching on life.

The Spiritualist Movement will be left behind unless there is an infusion of new teaching, just as in the case of the Swedenborgian Movement.

Here is the archetypal plan: From God, through the Archons, through the Great Angels, through the souls of just men made perfect, through the Adepti, who live in seclusion, to the people.

The Spiritualist Movement is the bridgehead. We propose to send the new impulse through this channel, if it is open.

C: Certainly the channel is open because I am.

N: Your credentials were not asked for because we put you there and can keep you there. But remember this: "Above all - no zeal." Zeal generally means indiscretion.

Practical matters:

This nation occupies a position of great importance in the spiritual history of mankind; it is worthy to be worked through. What is needed is a clear-cut formulation to the national mind. Therefore explanation, teaching and instruction are necessary for intelligent cooperation. The Occult Movement needs contact with the public mind; we offer you our cooperation.

C: I am very glad to accept that cooperation. There is a conflict between ignorant belief and the higher teaching.

N: Yes, they worship the dead. You have to cleave the rock along the line of cleavage. Certain teaching will be given you from the higher planes; you must present it to your readers in a digestible form. Loyalty can be used; there may be faith if not discernment. There have been some communicators in the past above the average, such as "Imperator". The communications differ in degree but not in kind.

The teaching must be published as from an unknown communicator through an unknown medium. The communications must be judged on their intrinsic value. It will be considered a privilege to meet an unknown medium and an unknown communicator.

[There followed an unrecorded discussion as to the name under which the communications were to be printed, and a reference by C to arousing opposition.]

N: Explain that the communicator wishes to be nameless, and a name being necessary, you will refer to him as "The Nameless". You met the medium by invitation but you are pledged to secrecy.

The communications of a new communicator will be valuable to the paper.

C: I would prefer personal contact at the beginning.

N: There will be a great amount of material. It will be taken down by those accustomed to take down communications. The matter dealt with will be national and world conditions; not in reference to politics but to first principles which constitute the philosophy of politics; trends and lines of development. We teach and transmit power. Those who align themselves with the teaching get power. We never touch on practical politics. We can tell you what will happen but not when. I will also deal with questions in order to strengthen your position with your readers. Here are a few minor points:

There is no question as to the outcome of the war, only how long it will last. This depends on how quickly men can win to certain realisations and give them effect. A new epoch is opening, called in the common parlance of the Mystery Schools, the Aquarian Age.

The Aquarian Age will see a great change in social organisation. The social unit or nation will become much more highly organised; there will be closer and greater centralised control; and individuals will have to contribute much more of individual existence to the common whole than in the past. The problem will be to obtain a high degree of individualisation with a closely integrated social organisation. This will only be possible by the intelligent co-operation of the individual units forming the nation. To this end the general educational level of humanity must be greatly raised. The whole standard of living must be liberalised, because degraded human beings cannot exercise sound judgement.

The democratic principle will survive because it is the only form of organisation that permits of a high degree of development in individuals. Equally, the efficiency of a democracy depends on a high grade of development in the individuals composing it.

The Piscean Age, which is passing, saw the development of the individual ego through the influence of Christianity, to which each soul is sacred; and the Aquarian Age will see the development of highly organised and integrated social systems, built out of highly developed individuals.

The masses must delegate an efficient authority to enable agreed schemes to be carried through. Government must always be by the consent of the governed if individual development is to be achieved, but the governed must consent to be governed efficiently and must bring an instructed understanding to the political task.

Autocracy will always destroy individuality in all save the governing class and will consequently deprive itself of a rising generation of leadership, and so die off at the centre.

The evidence of this statement is to be sought in history.

One other point for your readers; for this I can offer no evidence; it is merely fact as known to me:

In the past there have been holy centres where spiritual forces have come through to the world of men: Rome, Jerusalem, Thebes and Lhasa have been such centres. The centre for the new age will be London.

[With reference to the title of the new series of articles the title was left to C but was to be submitted to N before use.]

Deferring to scepticism is a waste of time. Scepticism is of the mind. Driving force is of the emotions. As a journalist you must speak to the heart rather than to the head. Stress the emotional and imaginative aspects.

From a journalistic point of view the idea of London as a spiritual centre is more attractive than political forecasts.

Humble people want a sense of their own value. Never despise them; respect sincerity; remember limitations of understanding. Therefore teach simply but with authority. Remember that it is the credulous who give hospitality to new ideas.

Simply ignore the quarrelsome and vain. "Great is truth and it shall prevail."

Remember your own trade. You must have the human touch; the great body of people need concrete images not abstract philosophy. Your intellectuals will not accept this widespread teaching. The common people need hope and self-respect from feeling they can play their part; recognise their limitations but respect their sincerity.

Both sides should be fostered in "Light" at the same time. You will have the higher teaching plus something that appeals to the imagination; then the intellectuals will respect and the simple will venerate.

You will announce a nameless communicator and an unknown medium; this will attract the simple and the intrinsic quality of the communications will appeal to the intellectuals.

The work must be broad based on the masses. For them we must be somewhat dogmatic but we can give reasons for the dogma.

A word of warning. Against us there are organised and intelligent forces which are *not* serving Cosmic Law. The medium is protected by secrecy. You are out in the open and your service is not without danger. Ask if you need protection; there is power behind this work.

It is a game of rival influences on the ignorant and susceptible.

As a man of sense you will naturally take no notice of anonymous communications. You will want my credentials. I will not turn tables. You will get what you need in a sense of power, and an inner sense of reality. "I speak not with my own authority but on behalf of the Great ones who transmit God's will, God's wisdom." You will remember the record in the New Testament of the two disciples who, after speaking with one whom they supposed to be the gardener, said: "Did not our hearts burn within us?" That is the great test. And you will have a sign in spiritual growth of character.

As a result of these meetings Cammell no doubt felt convinced that "Light" could be an important vehicle for higher teaching in the days that lay ahead if he were allowed to implement this policy.

"Light" was (and still is, now a quarterly journal of the College of Psychic Studies) primarily a spiritualist publication, although its banner heading in 1942, when it was still a weekly newspaper, read *"A Journal of Spiritualism, Psychical, Occult and Mystical Research - Founded 1881"* which suggests that in former times its editorial policy had embraced a wider spectrum of esoteric interests.

That of course was the time when "Imperator", a spirit communicating through the unlikely channel of the Reverend Stainton Moses, (writing psuedonymously originally under the pen name MA(Oxon), a well educated public school master), began to make a considerable stir in esoteric circles. Hitherto spirit communications had tended to be vapid and sentimental but "Imperator" turned out to be a consistent and intelligent Neo-Platonist who in the end even converted his amanuensis out of his somewhat rigid Victorian establishment theology. It is to be remarked that "Imperator" is singled out for remark by Dion Fortune's communicator, just as he had been initially hailed as a significant break through by Madame Blavatsky and her mahatmas, as may be seen in her "Isis Unveiled" - even if the honeymoon period did not last, as may be read in "The Mahatma Letters to A.P.Sinnett."

The ground was elaborately prepared for future teachings, and C.R.Cammell devoted three editorials, of January 15th, February 5th and February 26th 1942, gently introducing them to his readership.

On January 15th, under the heading of "Unusual Communications", he announced that it had been his recent privilege to obtain certain trance communications of an unusual character, and that the medium was a person *"of high literary distinction, whose remarkable psychic gifts had never been employed professionally and were known only to a small and strictly limited number of friends, each of whom was a serious student of the occult and spiritual sciences."* He then gave almost verbatim the text of the trance of November 1941 that we have quoted above, with particular emphasis on the possibility of London being a future spiritual centre for the post-war age.

It is apparent from Cammell's editorial of 5th February that he had experienced some opposition to this new source of teaching, either from the readership or the management. Indeed there is interesting corroboration that this might be the case in a note in the Society of the Inner Light's archives, where a series of trance messages received by Dion Fortune on 14th February 1942, include the statement: *"Tell CRC that organised opposition is at an end. He should strive to reconcile himself with those who opposed him, but there is one woman, the centre of the opposition, who will probably prove irreconcilable."*

In his editorial of February 26th 1942, under the heading "Mediumship explained from Beyond," Cammell published most of the text of the October trance. A text which, as we have seen, was extremely practical, rather than occultly philosophical.

Despite the earlier strictures over not revealing the source of these communications, Dion Fortune's name finally appeared publicly in "Light" on 23rd April 1942, as author of a major article entitled "The Secret Tradition," that was serialised over three issues.

The Secret Tradition

Occultism and Spiritualism

Let me commence by answering the very reasonable question: what have spiritualists to do with the Ancient Wisdom? More than most of them realise, for occultism is traditional spiritualism. Whether we study the Delphic Oracles or the witch trials of the Middle Ages, we encounter authentic psychic phenomena. Spiritualists would find themselves on familiar ground if they penetrated to the caves of Tibet or the temples of Ancient Egypt, for the Secret Tradition has been built up by generations of psychics and spirit controlled mediums. The antagonism between modern occultism and spiritualism arose owing to the tendency of two of the trade to differ somewhat drastically. Followers of the ancient wisdom religion saw unauthorised trespassers investigating their preserves, and were neither helpful nor polite. Mme Blavatsky and MacGregor Mathers, the principal modern exponents of the Eastern and Western Traditions, both decried mediumship; but Mme. Blavatsky was herself a medium, and a very fine one, as witness *The Mahatma Letters*; and MacGregor Mathers made use of the mediumship of his wife, sister to Henri Bergson, in reconstructing the rituals of his famous "Order of the Golden Dawn." I cannot speak concerning what goes on nowadays in the Esoteric School of the Theosophical Society, but mediumship and clairvoyance were to my knowledge made use of in the higher grades of the "Golden Dawn," the deprecation of these practices by occultists being of the nature of a smoke screen. Initiates of the lesser grades may take these denials seriously, but those who are acquainted with the practical work of the higher grades know what value to set on them. While I am entirely in agreement with a policy of caution in developing gifts that are by no means without their attendant risks and drawbacks, I am not prepared to endorse deliberate mis-statements. Spiritualism and occultism are much closer akin than spiritualists realise or occultists will admit.

The occult tradition is a vast storehouse of spiritualistic experience, handed down through the ages from initiator to candidate in the ancient ceremonies, which are, when properly understood, methods of psychic development. Out of this mass of visions, phenomena, and spirit teaching a very wonderful philosophy and cosmogony has been developed, identical in its essence all the world over and in all ages, but always expressed in the terminology of the religion of the time and place. An even more wonderful system of psycho-physiology has also been developed and applied to practical purposes of which the uninitiated have little idea. Although no upholder of occult secrecy in regard to the philosophy and cosmogony, I share the view that discretion should be observed in disclosing the occult psycho-physiology just as in the dispensing of drugs, because of the practical applications to which it can be put, and the fact that these can be abused by unscrupulous persons.

Serious students of the occult use considerable reserve in imparting their knowledge, some key piece usually being held back. Their fellow initiates, knowing what these factors are, can supply the missing parts, thus rendering the knowledge capable of practical application. Those who are not initiates can share in the philosophy but are unable to participate in the actual practice of the occult processes. There are innumerable occult societies, large and small - mostly small - scattered up and down the country, working in conditions of more or less strictly observed secrecy; some possessing the missing keys and others not even knowing that they exist; some having a high mystical aim or engaged in valuable research into the little-understood powers of the mind-side of nature, while others are just foolish mutual admiration societies, or make use of hallucinative drugs and orgiastic rituals. Sometimes the traditional secrecy is maintained in the spirit of children playing at Indians; sometimes it is used as a cloak for subversive political activities. Anyone venturing into the occult field does well to test each step lest he set foot in a morass.

The principal source of trouble is the secrecy, which prevents the useful sharing of knowledge and the wholesome criticism of methods. The solution of the problem cannot, owing to the nature of occult work, be solved by the wholesale application of publicity. The initiate, engaged in the practical experimental work which is called magic in occult circles and psychic phenomena in spiritualistic ones, knows by experience that he must work with carefully selected people if he is to get good results. His working is apt to be more easily disturbed than the working of a psychic developed by spiritualistic methods, because his technique is more intricate and elaborate, being enshrined in traditional rituals. Personally, I think that occultists could profit by an acquaintance with the method of developing mediums used in well conducted "home circles", which would enable them to cut away a great deal of the traditional ritualistic paraphernalia. All the same, the ancient sonorous rituals are exceedingly impressive when well done, and enable people to share inspiring psychic experiences at first hand, who would have to depend on the mediumship of others when investigating by the spiritualistic method.

Occult methods, moreover, give access to an aspect of the Unseen which has been little explored by spiritualists, who are mostly concerned with the problems of survival. There are great spheres of angelic and elemental existence awaiting investigation. The occultist concentrates for the most part on these and concerns himself not at all with the proof of survival, which he takes for granted. He does, however, investigate the data of reincarnation and destiny - or karma, to give it the better known Eastern term, that sums up the influence of past lives on the present.

Occultism possesses an immense amount of traditional data concerning the nature of the aura, or subtle body - certain little understood powers of the human mind, and the even less known "mind side" of nature. All these have practical applications in mystical philosophy, psychotherapy, and even the affairs of nations, of which we have but touched the fringe. Owing to the traditional secrecy of the occult movement, and the exclusiveness of all its component units, the practical development of this knowledge lags lamentably. There is, however, a movement towards a rapprochement in occult circles, a pooling of data and experience, which could lead to very valuable results if pursued generously and in good faith. If the spiritualist societies joined in this movement its value would be immeasurably enhanced, for the two viewpoints could supplement and countercheck each other.

Such a co-operation, however, can only develop where mutual knowledge has led to mutual confidence. The occultist is usually a person of an intellectual type, with some knowledge, and sometimes a profound knowledge, of the psychology of the subconscious mind and comparative religion; he is not interested in proving survival as he probably remembers his own past lives and so has the best possible evidence in first hand experience. Nor is he usually the type of person who appreciates advice from departed relatives. The things that are all-important to those making their first steps out of materialism or blind faith are taken for granted by him and he is apt to be impatient of their demonstration, forgetting that other people have other needs and everything must have a beginning. He has also heard a good deal about fraudulent Mediums.

The spiritualist, on the other hand, has probably heard a good deal about necromancy, orgiastic rituals, sex magic, vision inducing drugs that lead to addiction and some pretty dubious characters among the adepts. To all this I reply that if the spiritualist will admit that fraudulent mediums do exist, I will admit that black occultists exist also; but I think we may mutually agree that reputable organisations in both camps make short work of such individuals, and that their sporadic occurrence is not sufficient justification for refusing to investigate that vast sphere of existence collectively called the Unseen.

The Occult Movement Today

The Secret Tradition presents at first sight an enigmatic appearance, so that the investigator is tempted to remark with the Mad Hatter, "Jam yesterday, and jam tomorrow, but never jam today." One reads of marvels in far off countries and far off times, whereas the present time and the present place are miserably matter of fact. Or one may meet students of the occult and find them either poseurs or painfully credulous. To a cursory examination the occult is either non-existent or unprepossessing. A great deal of very clap-trap literature has been published on the subject. The public for such books is small, therefore they are not a paying proposition for a publisher, and unless the author is prepared to take a financial risk, will not appear in print. Consequently, a good many books appear that would never have seen the light of day on their own merits.

The deeper occult teaching circulates in manuscript form among small groups of people pledged to secrecy. It is a great pity that the occult teachers, even if they consider it undesirable to make their teaching available to an unselected public, should not pool it among themselves; but the tradition of secrecy is so ingrained in the movement that it is not easily abrogated. Moreover, people are generally bound to this secrecy by traditional oaths concerning which nobody seems to have the power to give dispensation, even when such oaths have been made ridiculous by the advance of popular knowledge. When I was initiated I swore to keep secret from all uninitiated persons the methods of the Hebrew Numerical Qabalah, that curious technique for the interchanging of numbers and letters to yield magical formulae, upon which nowadays several scholarly books are available. I also swore to keep secret certain astrological data which modern astrologers would consider a first course for beginners.

The occult dove-cots, however, were badly fluttered a few years ago when the secret papers of one of the most famous of the occult fraternities, the "Golden Dawn," were published in four volumes in America; but any one who reads these books in the hope of learning the occult secrets will be sadly disappointed, for they are quite incomprehensible to the outsider, though an invaluable encyclopaedia of reference for the initiated. I had all this material in my possession many years ago, laboriously copied by hand. I had to learn it off by heart in order to pass the tests of the grades; no explanation was ever given me concerning its real rationale and use - these are Lost Secrets in the "Golden Dawn" today; but a very old, bed ridden woman gave the key when she whispered in one of her rare intervals of consciousness - "Study Yoga and the methods of the spiritualist circle." It was in the light of this hint, and my previous knowledge of psycho-analysis, that I was able to find my way through the Valley of Dead Bones to which I had been admitted by virtue of my initiation.

Yoga, spiritualism, and the psychology of the unconscious are the three keys that open the gates of the Ancient Mysteries to modern thought. The Yoga methods are based on a great body of practical experience concerning the anatomy, physiology and culture of the etheric double, and would well repay the attention of those seeking psychic development. Concerning spiritualistic methods, I should not presume to speak in these pages, save to acknowledge my indebtedness for many practical hints I have picked up therefrom, and to recommend the technique of the developing circle to the attention of occultists who want to find out why, with them, it is seldom "jam today." The more advanced occultists and spiritualists are nowadays well aware of the value of modern psychology in counter-checking psychic experiences; perhaps the day is not distant when psychologists will realise what the psychic sciences could give them in the way of data and technique.

Occult organisations vary enormously in both the quality and quantity of their teachings; and though they are in general agreement as to first principles, differ widely in their practical methods. There is no secrecy nowadays about the occult philosophy - it is published in innumerable books; but the practical technique is carefully guarded by each organisation, partly on grounds of the traditional secrecy and partly as a trade secret of value in competition with rivals. These methods consist firstly in the knowledge of the ancient symbols and their use, though it is not infrequent to meet with teachers who know the symbols but don't know their use.

The practical methods employed fall into the two divisions of meditation and ritual. Some schools use one, and some use the other, but worthwhile results, in my opinion, are only obtained in schools that combine the two. First the student is taught the symbol system and its implications; then he is taught how to concentrate his mind in meditation upon the symbols in the proper sequence; and finally, he is shown how these symbols are combined into formulae in the ceremonial workings. There are groups that possess the heritage of fine traditional systems, but know nothing whatever of their meaning and have only a rule of thumb, hit or miss, conception of their use; there are psychics who, knowing nothing of traditional occultism, have become possessed of its practical technique by means of their powers and make good use of it.

For many years I have inveighed against occult secrecy as not only outworn but dishonest; more and more clearly has widening knowledge taught me the value of a rapprochement between occultism and spiritualism, and I am convinced that the time is now ripe for such a development. I, from occult sources, have received intimations to that effect, and I shall be interested to see whether spiritualists are receiving similar intimations from their own guides and spirit friends.

The Method of Occult Science

It is not easy to convey a fair and adequate conception of occultism to readers meeting it for the first time. There are two kinds of truth in this field of thought - the familiar, objective truth of the physical plane founded on sensory data, and the unfamiliar, subjective truths of the Inner Planes of subjective consciousness, depending on relative degrees of awareness, in which what is true for one person is untrue for another. Herein we can neither accept things at their face value nor stigmatise them as lies. Confusion results when the two planes of existence, the sensory and the subjective are confused. What has been known empirically to occultists since first there was any occult science worthy of the name, has at length been formulated scientifically by Einstein in his doctrine of relativity. Into its intricacies I will not attempt to go, but will content myself with reminding my readers that time and space may be conceived as modes of consciousness, and that we consider them absolute and arbitrary only because all our minds work in the same way. Change the adjustment of the mind, and the perception of experience changes with it. This is an important clue to the nature of supernormal phenomena. I do not want to embark upon abstruse philosophical discussions in these pages, but would like to indicate to my readers where they may look for confirmation of what I have to say, for in order to be brief I must be dogmatic, though I have always considered dogmatism to be intellectual impudence, and have no wish to commit that breach of scholastic manners.

We must always be prepared, in studying occult philosophy for two modes of approach, one of which considers that things exist in their own right and affect us by reason of their intrinsic qualities, and the other which considers that all we know of existence is our own reaction to it, and that if we change the focus of consciousness we change the nature of experience; nevertheless such adjustment is not arbitrary, but might be likened to the squaring or cubing of a number in mathematical calculations - the nature of the number remains unchanged though of a higher potency.

It is well known that primitive peoples are much more psychically and emotionally sensitive than civilised ones, whose education tends to concentrate consciousness on the intellectual processes to the neglect of the subtler capacity that passes under the name of intuition.

It is not perhaps so well realised that the artistic temperament approximates very closely to the primitive type, for it works in a manner that can well be described as psychic in relation to the particular art in which it finds expression; the artist, however, whether in sound, form and colour, or words, needs in addition to his power of intuitive apprehension a highly developed intellect that he can bring to bear on this chosen sphere, if he is to be a great artist. The same considerations apply in psychic matters; there are psychics who are simply primitive sensitives with no critical faculties, and there are sensitives whose natural psychism works through the vehicle of an intellect developed by the discipline of philosophy. There are also initiates whose intellectual powers have at their service psychic faculties developed by certain technical methods based on a knowledge of the psychology of the unconscious mind and magnetic field that surrounds and interpenetrates the living body and which is commonly called the *aura*. The practical application of occultism, popularly known as magic, is concerned with the development and utilisation of these two little understood factors in the human make-up.

The occultist has at his disposal an immense mass of traditional data; chaotic, fragmentary, and mostly recorded by scholars who had no idea what it meant. Take the jargon of alchemy, for instance; it is simply the psychology of psychic and spiritual development expressed in symbolic terms; if its terms are understood, its meaning becomes clear. Intermingled with the true tradition, however, are masses of spurious speculations by men who did not possess the real keys and were guessing more or less wildly at their nature and whereabouts; mistaking spiritual gold for the precious metal, they hoped to make their fortunes out of it, with results that can readily be guessed. Those who remember the rumours that were current in the last war, and to a lesser degree in this, will have no difficulty in assessing the history of alchemy at its true worth if they bear in mind that its historians have never been its initiates. It is as if a history of England were compiled from the utterances of Mr. de Valera and Lord Haw-haw by a Martian historian unacquainted with the physical conditions of this planet.

The Secret Tradition has had many ups and downs in the course of its long history owing to the fact that its deeper teachings cannot be set forth in plain words that the intellect can understand, but have to be arrived at intuitively by meditation on symbols, for the average human mind is not capable of apprehending them until after long and strenuous training. This training has to be graded systematically in order to avoid injury to the mind, just as in the case of the training of muscles in gymnastic exercises. Do I convey anything to my readers if I tell them that when the initiate reaches some of the higher grades in the Mysteries, he is shown an empty shrine as the symbol of the final revelation of the truth, even if I warn them not to jump to the conclusion that occultists are atheists? Yet it is only when the initiate grasps the significance of that empty shrine that he is able to wield the magic wand. Will I make the matter any clear if I offer the additional information that in a lower grade leading thereto the neophyte is shown a shrine with a mirror in it in which he sees his own reflection? Yet if you realise the significance of these two symbolic presentations of a great truth, and why they are placed in that order, you have the key to the practical working of the Mysteries.

It is obvious that in this Spring and Summer of 1942 considerable ebullience was felt by Dion Fortune in the future of the Mystery Tradition and of her group's part in it in particular. We find that a series of activities is announced in her circulated Weekly Letters to associates of the Fraternity.

On the 12th April the Guild of the Master Jesus began its Sunday services again, which had been abandoned at the outbreak of war. And on 20th April a series of Monday evening lectures was commenced. This included talks by members who had but recently joined the Society but who were destined for rapid progress and a subsequent controlling function in the post-war years. We see, for example A. Chichester giving a talk on "Entering upon our Heritage" and Mrs. R. Mann lecturing on "Magic". Other long standing members of the Fraternity also do their bit, the librarian Miss H.C.Brine, on "Merlin and Tintagel" and Miss Katherine Barlow on "Christianity & Magic" and also "Wisdom and Fairy Lore". Other talks covered "Occult Teachings in Daily Life" and "Suggestion and Auto-suggestion" and Dion Fortune would give the first Monday lecture in each month.

On 21st June the Chalice Orchard Hostel at the foot of the Tor at Glastonbury was re-opened for visitors, and from July 1st Dion Fortune embarked upon a fortnightly series of lectures at the headquarters of the Marylebone Spiritualist Association in Russell Square, that lasted through to 21st October.

Initiatives were also explored upon a more personal basis and we find the unusual circumstance of an occultist of Dion Fortune's calibre booking a consultation with a spiritualist medium, Mrs.Methuen, whose guide was known as "White Wing". Dion Fortune's account of this meeting has survived and seems worthy of reproduction here.

Interview with "White Wing", Red Indian Guide of Mrs. Methuen at the International Institute, August 31st 1942 at 2.30.

As the medium went into trance I saw an aura of pale orange light around her very distinctly. I saw this with the physical eyes, not by visualising, and it is the first time I have had this experience. The aura remained right throughout the sitting, fading towards the end, and then flaring up brightly for a moment as the medium came out of trance. When she moved from side to side in her chair, the aura remained in the same position, so that I saw more of it when she leant to one side than when she was right in the middle of it, and it appeared around her like the photosphere round the sun in total eclipse. At one point the control referred to an aura of gold and blue, and a few moments before she spoke I had seen an outer ring of blue appear in the aura above the medium's head and shoulders.

Before going to the sitting I had invoked my own guides, asking that a check-up might be made on my own psychism, for one of my chief troubles has been lack of self confidence, and the fear that I may be deluding myself and others owing to subconscious contents getting mixed with my psychism. The control dealt with this point at considerable length and very explicitly, giving me much valuable advice and reassurance, of which I was much in need.

He proceeded point by point to deal with the topics on which I had recently been having counsel and instructions from my own controls, thus counterchecking them in a very interesting and evidential manner. I had intended to take notes, but passed into a psychic state myself, and did not wish to disturb this, so must rely on memory. I am not giving the points in the order in which they were dealt with, but the more salient points are clearly registered in my memory, and no doubt one will lead to another as I proceed to write them down.

White Wing told me that I had much psychic power, a great mission to perform, and would receive great help from the inner planes, more than I realised or was ready to avail myself of. He described accurately the difficulties I had encountered in life, and should continue to encounter, but said I had ample help from the inner planes to enable me to drive through them. I have always been conscious of this, and have often likened myself to a ship driving through a heavy sea with decks awash, but coming up after each plunge. White Wing used the metaphor of the ship, but said a new phase was opening for me, and I was coming into smoother water. This also I have been told by my own Master.

He said that though much of my work was done in secret, I was to come out into the open after September and speak to the populace, and that help would be given me if I stood forth boldly. He described me as standing on a high platform, semi-circular, so that I had to turn from side to side to speak to the people around me. This applies well enough to the hall in which I hope to speak, for though the platform is rectangular, it is exceptionally high, the hall is semi-circular, so that I have to turn from side to side in addressing my audience, a feature somewhat unique in public halls, where the audience is usually in front of one, and not round at the sides as well. I therefore consider this point interesting and evidential.

The medium, before going into trance, described with accuracy the appearance and dress of my principal guide. White Wing described two Tibetans who came and said they were teachers who wished to give me teaching. One of these I saw very clearly over her right shoulder, but not the other. Later White Wing said that one of the two Tibetans gave a name that sounded like Mureed, and said that he particularly wished to work with me. I was also conscious of having very definitely picked up this contact. Tibet has had a great attraction for me, and I have read about it extensively and feel that I know it very well.

White Wing further gave me a message from an Egyptian priest who had worked with me in an Egyptian temple during one of the earlier dynasties. He said this entity wished to work with me as he had worked with me before. There has been an Egyptian priest, who has been seen by several clairvoyants, coming and going rather erratically for several years in both my astral journeys and as my control. It was quite clear to me that this was the entity referred to, for the wording of the message referring to past work done together gave me the necessary clue to identify him. I feel that I have also been able to establish this contact.

Advice was given me to get into touch with the inner planes late at night. I have been in the habit of doing this in the afternoon hitherto, avoiding late night work as liable to prevent sleep, but will try out the advice and see how it works.

White Wing then said that Mrs. Besant was present and very anxious to speak to me, and gave me a message from her. Mrs. Besant said that she had left work undone when she died which she was anxious that I should carry on. This fitted in very curiously with an impulse, which had come to me strongly and repeatedly during the past few days to get in touch with the Theosophical Society. I had been hesitating about this, as I have no reason to expect a cordial welcome in that quarter, having criticised its leaders severely over the World Teacher movement and certain scandals arising out of the methods of magical work taught in a certain inner section. The T.S. had retaliated in no uncertain manner. I said that I would act on my impulse to make the contact if Mrs. Besant would take steps to prepare the way; this she said she would do, and warned me to persevere even if the response was not very good at first. I had not mentioned anything of the opposition I expected to encounter, so regarded the warning as evidential. Moreover, a few days before, a member of the T.S., a somewhat prominent one, whom I had known many years ago when I was in touch with that organisation, had turned up at one of my lectures. It was the first time I had made a Theosophical contact for a great many years, so although a minor point, and non-evidential by itself, taken in conjunction with the others, it is interesting.

White Wing described me as seated in a small room all hung around with gold draperies, and an entity, who she at first referred to as an angel, and then as man, engaged in protecting me. This would be a quite good description of the conditions under which I live, which are kept sealed and protected by magical means, a circle of gold light being drawn round them, and one of the members of my group having the task of "putting on the seals" daily. White Wing's uncertainty as to whether the entity seen was an angel or a man would no doubt be caused by the fact that the person concerned does the work in his astral body, and White Wing's uncertainty on this point is interesting as evidential. If he were not accustomed to the methods of working of initiates of the Western Esoteric Tradition, he would no doubt be puzzled by the use of astral projection by persons in the flesh.

He said that my work divided up into either five or seven classes or sections. Neither he nor I were very clear as to what this meant. I suggested it might refer to the grades of my organisation, which has three Lesser Mystery Degrees, and it is in my mind to organise two Greater Mystery degrees in the near future. That would explain the five divisions. There are also two other Rays we work, in addition to the Hermetic Ray above described, which are not divided into grades. This might account for the seven but this reference is not clear to me.

White Wing described accurately my relations with my parents, which have never been very helpful or sympathetic, and my separation from my husband; saying, in my opinion correctly, that neither of us desired to recontact the other, and would never do so, as our evolutionary paths would not touch again. He said that I had learnt much and taught much through the marriage relationship, and that I had done well. I was glad to hear this, as I had no means of assessing my own conduct objectively.

He said that there was some man working with me, aged about 65, who would want to marry me, but advised me against marriage as it would hamper my work, and to keep the relationship on a mental level. There are several men working with me, but no one of this age, nor who is in the least likely to fulfil this prediction. I had similarly received instructions from my own Masters with regard to remarriage.

White Wing said he saw a triangle over my head terminating in a globe of light. This is a symbol referring to the Lesser and Greater Mysteries.

He said further that I had begun recently to develop healing powers of which I was unaware, and should cultivate them; that there were doctors on the inner planes who wanted to work through me, and that I should read and experiment along these lines to as to make myself a suitable vehicle for this kind of work. He asked if I were not especially interested in breathing and similar exercises and the study of the aura. All this was quite correct. He advised me to make contact with people who were working along healing lines so that I might learn from them. This had also been impressed on me by my own teachers. The presence of healing power recently I had begun to suspect. My constitutional scepticism however had prevented me from trying to make use of it.

White Wing had much explicit advice to give me concerning an inferiority complex which he said robbed me of self confidence and prevented me from doing my best work. Of this I have long been very conscious, and his counsel and confirmation were very helpful to me.

He further promised to give me all the help and assistance that he could personally, because he thought my work important, and that it would be helped from the inner planes very strongly. He said that a number of Egyptian initiates now in incarnation would be drawn to me and help me with my work. This is probable, as we work on Egyptian contacts, among others; in fact they are the predominating ones. He further said that there were people who would sap my energy "like a leech", and that I should detach myself from them and not allow them to hamper my work. He repeated the expression "like a leech" several times. It is interesting to note that it had a very special and definite significance for me in this connection. He also said that I had erred through over generosity and too much kind heartedness. This was significant to me, for I am expecting to have claims made on my generosity in the near future. He advised keeping my energy and resources for my work, which is what I had made up my mind to do. It is very helpful, however, to have this confirmation, as it is difficult to judge righteous judgement where one's own interests are at stake.

White Wing was very definite that after the war was over I would go on a trip to America, but was not to settle there. Of this also I have had intimations. He thought it possible that I might visit India. He asked if I had ever been in India, as he had a strong sense of India about me. I have never been there on the physical plane, but of recent years have developed contacts with the Eastern Tradition and have been in the habit of coming and going on the astral a good deal.

Towards the end the trance began to grow lighter, as was indicated by the fading of the orange light behind the medium which I had been watching waxing and waning and swaying slightly all the time.

White Wing then came down from the higher contacts which we had been making hitherto, among the Masters of my own Order, to the more usual type of contacts with which spiritualists worked, and spoke of seeing a lady with grey hair and thin face and blue eyes who had had heart trouble. He thought it might be my mother or grandmother, but neither of these answered to that description. One of my initiators would answer to it, however, in all particulars, except that she had massive features. I did not get any sense of contact with this entity however.

The interview was characterised by the fact that White Wing was relaying from my own controls to me, and that there were very numerous points that checked and counterchecked with the communications I have had myself, and of which the medium naturally knew nothing, nor anyone else outside my inner group, where secrets are well kept. I found the interview very helpful; firstly by the stimulus to my own psychism it afforded, which was an extremely valuable experience to me; secondly, by the confidence it gave me in finding so close a check up on my own communications and methods. It is clear to me that Mrs.Methuen and myself use exactly the same methods. At the end of the interview I was exhausted, and cold, despite the heat of the day, so it is evident to me that I had supplied some psychic force. There was a strong and steady sense of power in the room all through the interview, and it faded out gradually at the end, with the final spurt, as I have already described. I judged that the medium had been in pretty deep trance.

I am very grateful to the Institute and Mrs. Methuen for having afforded me this very valuable experience.

Dion Fortune

It is not our place or intention to pass any judgmental remarks upon the quality of this séance. Plainly Dion Fortune was quite pleased with it, although with the benefit of hindsight it is apparent that predictions of future trips to America or India are wide of the mark insofar that Dion Fortune was to die in January of 1946. That she was to die of leukaemia has a certain macabre resonance however with the emphasis laid on having her energy sapped as by a leech, for leukaemia is a cancer of the blood. However, it is easy to read later events into interviews such as this, that may well not have been intended.

What is slightly surprising is Dion Fortune's remarks about her having a certain sense of inferiority, for by all accounts she was a very outgoing personality, at any rate to her students. Her feelings of possible inadequacy with regard to her psychic powers are, in our opinion a healthy sign, together with the tendency to scepticism. Where the latter does not inhibit results altogether it is to be discretely encouraged in the psychic field. I have known other mediums of very high quality indeed, such as Margaret Lumley Brown, express similar doubts as to the veracity and worth of their own psychism. In anyone of responsible intelligence it is obvious that subject matter coming through their own conscious or subconscious processes must always be suspect as possibly emanating from themselves. It is those psychics who think that they are God's infallible gift to the world who are likely to be the more inaccurate. It is to this tendency that we owe, I think, the several remarks pertaining to "evidence" or "evidential" in Dion Fortune's report.

The confidential arrangement between her unnamed Master and C.R.Cammell seems to be coming apart at the seams later in the year, when we find him writing on 8th July 1942 to say that, all things considered, he feels it would be better not to resume the séances, as on various counts he finds a lack of sympathy between the communicator's mind and his own. At the same time, however, he is quite impressed with a script on King Arthur that he has received, and finds it difficult to believe that it came from the same source, and indeed is publishing it in an "Arthurian number" of "Light", in the week of 20th July, along with an article by Lewis Spence and a ballad of his own entitled "The Return of Arthur".

We find also at the beginning of July the closing down of the Guild of the Master Jesus, apparently through lack of support, and an end of the Monday lectures. Dion Fortune, however, like "a ship driving through a heavy sea with decks awash", continued with her series of fortnightly lectures at the headquarters of the influential Marylebone Spiritualist Association from July through to October.

She also made a public announcement of her own mediumistic abilities in the first of a series of Monthly Letters to associates and friends of her Fraternity in October 1942. The Monthly Letters replaced the one page Weekly Letters that had been inaugurated when "The Inner Light" magazine fell victim to war time paper rationing in August 1940. The new Monthly Letter, several pages long, gave scope for more extended articles. In the first, subscribers read the following announcement:

The Mediumship of Dion Fortune

The mediumship of Dion Fortune has been a well kept secret within the Inner Group of the Fraternity, but it has recently been decided to make a secret of it no longer in order that certain of the teachings thus received may be made available for all who follow the Path.

There followed an address received through her mediumship, with the hope expressed that similar addresses and extracts from the same source would be available for future issues. There was a great wealth of unpublished material that had been received in this way, and which would be released for publication.

In the second of the Monthly Letters, for November 1942, a further trance communication under the title "The Modus Operandi of Trance Communications - Received through the Mediumship of Dion Fortune", gave technical information along these lines, and was in effect the second part of the trance address of 26th October 1941 which C.R.Cammell had featured in the 26th February 1942 editorial of "Light". It contained some additional material at the end however.

Are they to know how written questions are answered? If the answer causes their hearts to burn, the link is made. That is the test. Personal advice is seldom given. You are to judge. It is a question of the principles underlying a case with which we deal. For those who are high in the Mysteries things can be done to facilitate their work that could not be considered in the lower grades. Intervention from the higher planes concerns the nature of Destiny and whether they can co-operate intelligently. The laws of destiny are mastered by observance.

In regard to a written question, if you bring it to me from someone who is seeking instruction and I answer it, a link is established, and in due course that person may be accepted for personal instruction. The results are twofold. The teaching of the doctrine is one thing, and can be conveyed by the written word, but the power of the Presence is another thing, and the written word only partially conveys it.

Xxxxx is a man with mystical contacts, and illuminated. He is the holder of a position; he invoked, and "I am come in answer to his prayer." It is not only a matter of what practical services he can give, but a matter of his past incarnations and his contacts. Therefore do not consider it from a purely utilitarian point of view. You know the old story of the person who uses the magical words and is startled by the appearance of the spirit? This man, using a true formula, made contact; much or little may come of it, but he is entitled to his opportunity. Results are his affair. It is not your responsibility, nor mine. You and I are channels, not sources of contact. Deal with him as originally planned; make no difficulty; let the matter work itself out. Give him the opportunity as promised. What use he makes of it, or fails to make of it, is his affair. The man who gives the correct password and knocks at the Door of the Mysteries may not be refused, even if he gives them in ignorance. But in this case they were not given in ignorance, but in a moment of vision. Let that impulse then set going take its course. A man has more than one incarnation. "Give to him that asketh of you". I am thinking of the help he needs, which should be given to him without question. Consider him as a soul lost in a dark forest who will go down into grievous darkness if he cannot have a helping hand. You may have wondered at the form my help took; that, being arrogant, he met with arrogance. "With the froward I will show myself froward."

What is said is not forgotten, and it will do its work; for it is a law of my being that I may not deny truth, and truth takes the responsibility. I may often have occasion to say to people what they may not like; it is not for you to soften the blow or turn aside the surgeon's knife.

It is tempting to speculate whether this refers to the contact with the Editor of "Light". Be this as it may, in her Monthly Letter of December 1942 Dion Fortune wrote a long article putting forth her current views on Spiritualism, which indeed modify some of her published views of twelve years before in "Spiritualism in the Light of Occult Science" and "Through the Gates of Death".

The Fraternity of the Inner Light and Spiritualism

It is desirable at the present juncture to make clear to our members and friends the position of the Fraternity of the Inner Light with regard to Spiritualism. To those who have knowledge of both movements it is obvious that they are the two sides of the same coin. Spiritualism is empirical occultism, Occultism is traditional Spiritualism. The methods and tone of the two movements differ, the one being propagandist and the other exclusive. In the past both had their separate tasks to perform, and could only perform them separately. Occultism had to keep alive and increase our heritage of psychic knowledge, and Spiritualism had to introduce the same concepts to the popular mind in a form that could be appreciated by people whose past incarnations had given them no subconscious aptitude for understanding the invisible realities and who were making their first approach to the Path. Both movements were under the jurisdiction of the Great White Lodge, but were carried on by different groups of Masters on the Inner Planes and their servers and pupils on the physical plane.

Independent organisation was necessary, as the one movement aimed at the widest possible publicity in order to influence popular opinion, (which it has done successfully) and the other still needed to remain in seclusion till public opinion had undergone the preparation that was the work of the Spiritualist movement. During the last great war Spiritualism came into its own and accomplished its mission, and its contribution to human thought is now an accepted part of our culture. In this war Occultism is coming into its own in turn, consolidating the ground pioneered by Spiritualism.

The Masters of the Great White Lodge have given instructions to the Brethren charged with the direction of both movements that the time for cooperation has come, and the two movements are to make contact at their periphery, like two circles meeting and slowly blending. There will for a long while yet be much of the Spiritualist movement which has no tinge of the occult philosophy but limits itself to research into psychic phenomena and the proof of survival, furnishing enquirers with evidence and the bereaved with consolation. There will also be a certain proportion of Occultism, the Greater Mysteries, which will continue to function in seclusion because the world is not yet ready for it. But there will be an unbroken line of approach from the propagandist aspect of the Spiritualistic movement right through to the arcana of Occultism. Both movements will be enriched thereby; the vast, undeveloped wealth of tradition being placed at the disposal of Spiritualists, and the highly specialised gifts of psychics and mediums being made available for the work of practical Occultism.

Having thus explained the essential unity of the two movements, we also need to make clear the factors in which they differ, not through antagonism, but through specialisation. Spiritualism is concerned primarily with the task of bringing the subtler forms of existence into touch with the physical plane through the work of its mediums and psychics, whose development for this purpose has been the object of a vast amount of study and accumulated data of experience. Occultism, on the other hand, teaches those who pursue it to function on the Inner Planes themselves, and as these levels of manifestation are the planes of causation in respect of the physical plane, it is possible, within certain limits varying with the attainments of the individual, to influence conditions on the physical plane. No hard and fast line can be drawn between Spiritualist and Occult activities in these matters, for it is obvious to all who have any practical experience of both movements that they overlap, but broadly speaking, the two movements will be found to have differentiated along the lines described because they have specialised along those lines, not because their activities are mutually exclusive. That Occultism has owed much to mediumship is witnessed by the tradition of the Oracles and the well known life story of Madame Blavatsky; after whose death C.W.Leadbeater, her student, continued to keep open the lines of psychic communication. The lesser known history of MacGregor Mathers, the great English occultist, who used his wife as his medium, and of his collaborator, Brodie Innes, who was himself mediumistic, confirm the tradition.

The question is frequently asked as to whether the Fraternity of the Inner Light makes use of mediums and psychics, and whether Dion Fortune, its Warden, is herself a medium. Hitherto information has been refused on this point to all save those in the higher grades of its own organisation. The time has now come, however, to give an answer. The Fraternity trains its students, to begin with, in the philosophy of the Esoteric Tradition and in the practice of meditation. Advancing beyond this grade, they are developed psychically and taught how to enter the Inner Planes by the traditional Paths. Advancing further, they study the art of operating the astral forces. All members take their part in the skrying, (or clairvoyance) according to capacity, but are not encouraged to act as mediums for each other, as they are expected to go on to the Inner Planes themselves and make direct contact with the Masters, by means of the meditation methods by which they are trained. A line of direct communication is always kept open, however, but it is operated from the Inner Planes, and the members of the Fraternity do not sit for development in mediumship. Dion Fortune at present holds this office, which she took over from her predecessor and teacher, who likewise received it from his teacher, but individual members have from time to time, according to capacity, had experiences that have enabled them to test for themselves the Inner Plane contacts claimed for their Fraternity. These have also been counterchecked recently by mediums belonging to well known Spiritualist organisations.

The Fraternity has never used psychic phenomena as a proof of the validity of its teaching, knowing that these phenomena, like miracles, prove nothing save their own existence and that teachings must be judged by their intrinsic content. The lines of communication with the Inner Planes which are used by occultists are more sensitive than those used by Spiritualists, and more easily disturbed by adverse psychic influences; consequently their work has to be guarded by the traditional seclusion, and our friends must forgive us if there is a certain reticence about our reference to them. No doubt we shall in time profit by our contact with the Spiritualist movement to improve our technique and throw open more widely the doors of the Mysteries. At present we must feel our way and make haste slowly in practical matters involving a break with age-old tradition.

It may be as well to say a few words here concerning the use of ceremonial, which plays so important a part in Occultism but of which Spiritualism has hitherto only so far availed itself in a very minor degree. The arrangement of the sitters in a circle, the playing of soft music, the singing of hymns and the prayers of dedication and invocation commonly practised in home circles are ritual of a simple kind; but there are aspects of ritual little realised by those who have not seen them, and their beauty and power bring through manifestations which, if subjected to psychic investigation, should yield very interesting results.

At the present moment, with the war hampering all our activities and dispersing our trained personnel, it is difficult, in fact almost impossible, for us to work these rituals in a way that shall do them justice, and ceremonial badly done is a very undesirable thing; but when happier days come, and they are already showing signs of dawning, we look forward to developments from the sharing of the Occult and the Spiritualistic resources, and co-operation with other Occult organisations which shall enrich the field of human knowledge for all men, and not just for one secret fraternity. This can only come about through generosity and open mindedness on both sides. In some quarters we have met with these truly Christian qualities in an abundance that has led to most happy relationships; in others, they have been regrettably lacking. May we be allowed to say that if we are right in believing that it is the will of those Great Ones behind both movements that there should be brotherly co-operation between their respective servers, then those organisations that will not co-operate will find themselves left behind by the march of events, and that the wonderful influx of new life that is flowing down upon us all from the Inner Planes will be unable to penetrate channels that are closed to brotherhood.

We, for our part, are not set in our ideas; we want to learn as well as to teach. There are things I wrote of Spiritualism twenty years ago which, in the light of wider experience, I would not write today, and to cite these as evidence against me is to deny the possibility of human progress. I was trained in a rigid tradition, and it has taken many years to win to a position where I could stand on my own feet, beholden to none, and with none in a position to call me to account under the Oath of the Mysteries for my actions. That is now my happy position, and I offer and ask for the pooling of knowledge by all who have anything to pool. Only thus can knowledge advance, and there is no religion higher than the Truth. Loyalty to Truth ranks higher than loyalty to personalities. I am no believer in the right to enforce an oath in a spirit of exclusiveness and pride of possession. The occult fraternities may be proud of their long descent and gorgeous rites, but true wisdom is humble, and compassionate to human needs, and if in our secret archives we have, as I know we have, knowledge that could lead on to human betterment and relieve human suffering, we have no right to guard it as our secret heritage, but should make it available for all who need it.

Dion Fortune

PART TWO

THE PSYCHOLOGY, PHENOMENA & TECHNIQUE OF TRANCE

The Psychology of Trance Mediumship

The fact that a phenomenon is unusual does not justify its classification as either a fraud, a pathology, or a miracle. The phenomenon of trance has been known from earliest days of which history has any record. It is known today among primitive peoples and among the most highly developed spiritual communities. It is also known in certain diseased conditions, and can be produced at will by drugs. It is obvious, therefore, that we are dealing with a definite psychological state, and that it is not the product of phantasy or fraud.

Being a state of consciousness, it must be explicable in terms of psychology, and it must be possible to relate it to other states of consciousness and demonstrate the intervening transitional states. It must also be possible to explain it, to some extent at least, in terms of that which is already known, for it is not a thing apart; it has its congeners, as we have already seen.

It is said by occultists that the gift of natural mediumship is due to occult training in a previous life. Be that as it may, the schizophrenic or personality splitting tendency plays a part in a good many forms of psychopathology which have been exhaustively investigated and it is necessary to consider what the psychologists have to say on the subject, for as we have previously pointed out, and as cannot be too often reiterated or too strongly emphasised in connection with the study of psychic states, they are not things *sui generis*, but are an integral part of our mental make-up, and we ought to study all allied mental states in order to see what light they may thrown upon them. It is of far more service to occult science to be able to demonstrate the relationship between normal consciousness and super consciousness and explain it in terms of known and proven science, than to guard the psychic faculties as sacrosanct and make a religion out of them. Spiritual things are placed on a far firmer basis if spirit can be shown to be natural than if it has to be regarded as supernatural.

It is of course, always necessary to bear in mind the many pathological conditions which closely resemble trance - epilepsy, hysteria, diseases of the central nervous system, and last, but unfortunately by no manner of means least, the self-delusion which is first cousin to fraud on the one hand and hysteria on the other, but which cannot definitely be assigned to either because it contains an admixture of both. This, unfortunately is always with us, and renders the task of psychic investigation very difficult.

For the present, however, we will leave out of consideration all such unsatisfactory cases, and seek to establish an understanding of true trance which will serve as a standard with which to compare all pseudo-trances.

We shall find the analysis of consciousness employed by occultists exceedingly useful in enabling us to arrive at a definition and classification of trance, and we will therefore briefly recapitulate such aspects of it as concern our present subject.

A human being, according to the occultist, consists of two clearly differentiated aspects - a higher and a lower; the higher being immortal and eternal, subject to neither birth nor death, but evolving with the evolution of the universe; and the lower, mortal and temporal, built up upon the basis of the Higher Self in each incarnation, beginning with the rudiments of consciousness at birth, and disintegrating at death; its abstract essence being absorbed by the Higher Self, which, by means of a series of such incarnations, gradually evolves. The Higher Self is called the Individuality and the Lower Self is called the Personality, and as these terms are convenient, they must be borne in mind for the purposes of this argument.

The nucleus of consciousness is called the Ego, or spark of pure life essence, about which all the rest is organised. The Individuality consists of the Ego, the spiritual nature, and the power of abstract thought. The Personality consists of the concrete mind, which is built up out of sensory experiences in each incarnation; the emotional nature in its higher aspect, which relates to ideas; the emotional nature in its lower aspect, which relates to the instincts and senses; and the physical body itself, concerning which natural science knows so much and understands so little because it considers it apart from the different organised systems of consciousness which the occultist, not without justification, terms the subtle bodies.

Normally, all these types of consciousness are synthesised into a whole, which may aptly be likened to a chord of music that, to the unskilled ear, appears as a single sound, but which the ear of the trained musician can analyse into its component parts and detect the slightest impurity in any note composing it. Equally can the adept occultist, who has trained his mind, analyse the different levels of consciousness and use them independently.

It is the experience of the trained occultist which throws most light on the phenomena of trance, for by means of a carefully developed technique he does deliberately and voluntarily that which takes place automatically and below the level of consciousness in the naturally mediumistic person. We can, therefore, learn much if we examine the modus operandi of the occultist who has leant to go into trance.

Before proceeding any further, however, we must define our terms. The state of trance must be distinguished from other states in which normal consciousness is in abeyance, to which it bears resemblance.

A trance condition may be described as a transmutation of consciousness rather than an abolition of consciousness, such as occurs in coma. Anyone familiar with the phenomena of trance knows that there is not complete unconsciousness; a response can always be elicited. It is in the nature of the response that differentiation is found, for the response of the entranced person differs materially from that of the same person in his normal state.

We can distinguish three distinct types of trance by observing the nature of the response which is obtained from the entranced person. Firstly, there is a type of trance in which the subject is apparently perfectly passive, in a deeply cataleptic state; if, however, a determined attempt is made to rouse him, he will awaken as if from deep sleep, angry and indignant at the interruption, but responding *in propria persona*. That is to say, the response will come from his normal personality conscious of its surroundings.

In the second type of trance a response can be elicited much more readily; the subject will not be ruffled and upset by being spoken to, and will again reply *in propria persona*, but with this difference, it will be obvious from his reply that he is but dimly conscious of his surroundings, and that his attention is directed elsewhere and he is perceiving with senses other than those of his physical body upon a plane of existence which is not that material environment which he shares with the observers; though all the while he remains sufficiently in touch with his companions to be able to report what is passing before his inner vision.

In the third type of trance a response can also be elicited readily enough when once it has been fully established, but that which responds is apparently not the original owner of the body, but someone else.

The occultist declares that trance is due to a dissociation of the self. A separation has taken place, or been induced, between the different levels of consciousness described on a previous page; the lower self, being deprived of the directing intelligence of the Ego, becomes passive, devoid of initiative, and only reacting to stimuli according to ingrained habit.

The different types of trance, according to the occultist, are due to the fact that the dissociation has taken place at different levels of consciousness. In the first type of trance, the separation takes place at the line of demarcation between the physical body and consciousness as a whole. The physical body then continues with the merely vegetative life of the tissues, while the self functions as a complete human consciousness minus a physical body. This is the deepest trance of all, and somewhat rare in the trained occultist who is not naturally mediumistic, for he considers it a very risky practice, as it is always problematical whether the heart can be induced to take up its beat again. This is the method used by yogis when they allow themselves to be buried alive, and in the condition into which hibernating animals enter.

A certain degree of levitation has been observable in the cases with which I have been acquainted. Not sufficient to float the body spontaneously, but enough to make it very easy to lift. The teacher under whom I originally trained frequently made use of this form of trance, and I have many times had occasion to help lift his inanimate body while in this state, and was always struck by the lack of weight. On one occasion I was able, without any undue effort, to lift him single handed from the floor to the sofa.

This kind of trance we will call the *Trance of Projection*, because the Self as a whole is withdrawn from the physical body and functions independently. I have many times witnessed this phenomenon in the case of my own teacher, and have on several occasions been able to verify the fact that he had appeared at a distance in a well materialised form.

The second type of trance we will call the *Trance of Vision*, because in this case the soul does not withdraw from the body, but, inhibiting the physical senses, appears to open up the senses of superconsciousness which can perceive the subtler planes of existence.

In this case the occultist declares that the dissociation of consciousness takes place between the upper and lower aspects of the Personality, that is to say, the mentality which is built up in the course of the present incarnation. The instincts and passions, being those aspects of consciousness which relate specifically to material existence, are linked with the physical body, while those aspects of the Personality which are closest akin to the Higher Self, maintain their union with that Higher Self, and when the Ego, freed from the bondage of matter, becomes the predominating influence in the Self, they share in the expansion of consciousness which ensues.

In the third type of trance, which is called the *Mediumistic Trance*, dissociation takes place between the Personality and the Individuality; that is to say, the whole of the Self which has been built up by the experiences of the current incarnation is left to ensoul the body, while the Higher Self, as a whole, withdraws.

It is held by occultists that the Ego alone is the seat of consciousness, and that the Lower Self or Personality, deprived of the Ego, has no initiative, or centralised directing intelligence, but simply consists of an elaborate co-ordination of reaction complexes, stereotyped by habit, which are capable of responding to their accustomed stimuli by their habitual reaction, but are without initiative, or intelligent adaptability.

In the Mediumistic Trance, we have, then, the whole Personality as we know it, minus the directing intelligence. The engine of consciousness is there. The engineer is absent.

It appears possible, however, for others than the original owner to lay hands on the levers and operate the machine. The mind with its knowledge of language, the body with its co-ordinated mechanism, are at the disposal of any ego that cares to manipulate them if the original owner stands aside.

What is it that takes place under such circumstances? How are we to explain an occurrence which diverges so widely from our usual experience of the nature of human personality?

The psychologist declares that what he calls dissociation of personality, or schizophrenia, has taken place, and secondary personalities have been formed by means of certain mechanisms well known to psychopathology. The occultist replies: I grant you that cases such as you describe do occur, but this case, though comparable to them, is not identical with them.

A case of schizophrenia is due to a complete break occurring in the stream of consciousness, a break so complete that no shred of memory extends across the gulf. Consequently, the incoming impressions cannot associate themselves with any existing memories because there are none, so a fresh start has to be made. A fresh personality is built up. For a personality, after all, is only a co-ordinated system of memories.

In schizophrenia, new Personalities are built up upon the nucleus of the same Individuality. But in mediumistic trance, different individualities take possession of the same Personality.

The essence of trance, then, is the withdrawal of the Ego from the physical body, leaving behind it varying amounts of the lower consciousness, and the different types of trance are due to the different amounts of consciousness remaining behind. The unconsciousness, be it noted, is only apparent; the body is inert because the Self is withdrawn, but the Self is fully conscious upon the plane to which it goes, though unaware of what transpires in connection with its physical body.

The reason that, for many trance mediums, trance appears to be a time of complete unconsciousness, is because the memory of what happens in the higher consciousness has no connecting links with ordinary consciousness and so can never be called to mind, just as a poem of which the first line is forgotten persistently eludes the memory. Keep the association chain intact or re-establish it, and the memories can be recovered. The occultist employs certain devices to maintain an association chain of ideas between the higher and the lower consciousness, and thereby he can prevent his memories of the experiences he undergoes in trance from being lost. He therefore has no sense of having been unconscious while in trance, though if withdrawal from the physical body has been at all complete, he will have no memory of what has transpired on the physical plane during the trance.

Under certain conditions, however, it is possible to remain in touch with the physical body, but the study of these conditions must be put aside until we have further considered the phenomena of trance consciousness, for at the present state of our inquiry we are not in a position to assess them.

The Physical Phenomena of Trance

An ounce of experience is notoriously worth a pound of theory, so before proceeding with any speculations as to the nature of trance, it will be advantageous to describe what exactly happens, or is experienced, when a person goes into trance.

I would not wish to be thought to speak dogmatically on this subject, for different schools of psychic development have different methods; I can only speak of that which I myself have seen and experienced; but I believe that that which I describe is substantially true, as to general principles, of all trance mediums, though differences in detail undoubtedly differentiate even between those psychics who have been developed in the same circle. No two persons taking an anaesthetic have precisely the same experience, yet the process of anaesthesia is well understood. So it is with trance mediumship. The psychology of trance is the same in all mediumship, whether natural or acquired.

As has already been said, the mental processes of trance can be more readily studied and analysed in the person who has acquired the power of mediumship by means of training than in the one who has it naturally; for the processes of the natural medium are so swift that they are exceedingly difficult of observation and analysis. Moreover, unless he has been drilled in the technique of psychological observation, his introspections will have little value.

The description upon which we are about to embark is of the nature of a slow motion film; it has been pieced together out of innumerable experiences, one point being noted here, another there; pondered over, pieced together, and experimented with for over ten years, in a ceaseless endeavour to make psychic experience fit in with psychological studies, holding steadfastly to the dictum that truth cannot contradict truth, but only requires to be correctly formulated in order to be correlated.

All three types of trance start in the same way, and consist of a withdrawal of consciousness from the objective world in order that the Ego may be freed from the limitations of the physical senses and the brain and enter upon independent activity upon its own plane.

The person who desires to use the subtle senses which belong to the higher states of consciousness is in the position of someone who wants to use the telephone while a gramophone is playing in the same room. In order to be able to hear the comparatively faint sounds of the telephone, he has to stop the gramophone.

In order to perceive the subtle impressions due to the reaction of the different types of consciousness to the conditions of their own separate modes of existence, it is necessary to inhibit the stronger impressions of the physical senses. This is done by shifting the focus of consciousness from the objective sphere to the subjective sphere.

In order to achieve this all important occult operation, the occultist concentrates with such intensity on the subjective world that all attention is withdrawn from sense impressions. It is for this reason that a trance medium usually requires a darkened room of an even and rather high temperature. Anything which attracts attention to the objective world tends to prevent the concentration of attention on the subjective world, and so inhibits trance.

The first stage of trance, then, consists of the withdrawal of attention from the objective world. It is for this reason that it is desirable to eliminate all external distraction as far as possible. It is not, of course impossible to go into trance under conditions of considerable disturbance, but only the very experienced medium can do so, and the results are apt to be so unsatisfactory that it is generally reckoned to be inadvisable to attempt it; complete withdrawal of consciousness does not take place, and the subconscious content gets mixed with superconsciousness.

The first physical sign to become apparent is a change in the rhythm of the breath; a few deep, sighing respirations are followed by a complete stoppage of breathing for a few seconds, and then respiration begins again with a different rhythm, shallow, slow, and from the diaphragm only; the ribs seem to play no part in it. Respiration, in fact, seems to be reduced to a minimum. This fact appears to relate trance mediumship to yogi breathing, as a change in the breath rhythm plays an important part in inducing changes of consciousness and aiding deep meditation. Moreover, the minimal nature of the respiration must certainly induce oxygen starvation in the blood, and we know that oxygen starvation of the brain is the reason for loss of consciousness in syncope. It is probable, therefore, that the reduction of the oxygen supply to the brain renders the perception of sense impressions less vivid, and so makes it easier for the Ego to withdraw. Be that as it may, it will be found that unless special care is taken to keep a trance medium warm, he will awake from his trance feeling chilled to the bone.

It is not easy to do physiological experiments on a medium who is entranced without breaking the trance and so vitiating the results, but on one occasion it was possible for a doctor to keep a stethoscope on the chest of a person who was going into trance, and he reported that all chest sounds ceased entirely for a time, and then continued very faintly. This indicates that definite physical changes do accompany trance, which is what we should expect according to both natural and esoteric science, and gives us a valuable means of distinguishing genuine from simulated trance.

The next physical sign to be noticed, and one which supervenes rapidly upon the change in the breath rhythm, is a peculiar spasm of the throat muscles, contracting and relaxing several times in succession as if trying to swallow a lump. This undoubtedly is closely related to the well known phenomenon of globus hystericus, so common in neurotics. It is said by occultists to be caused by the closing down of the thyroid gland, whose secretion is suspended during trance, for it is by the activation of the different chakras that the different levels of consciousness are opened up, and the chakras correlate exactly with the endocrine organs.

Rapidly upon the heels of the swallowing movement of the throat comes an unpleasant sensation in the eyes as if the eyeballs were being drawn upwards and inwards in a horrible squint, and immediately afterwards there is a sensation in the solar plexus such as is experienced in a rapidly descending lift. Then all sensations cease and the soul seems to be free of the body.

The body thus vacated becomes so rigid that it is possible to pick it up by the shoulders and ankles without its sagging. In all cases there is at least a momentary tensing of the muscles. In my experience of trance there has never been any limpness or relaxation. In fact so great is the tension of the muscles that unless precautions are taken to keep the knees flexed, they will become fixed and will be exceedingly painful to move after the trance is over.

It is held by occultists that the blood becomes very acid during trance; whether this is so or not I am not in a position to say, but it is noticeable that after trance the perspiration is sometimes of a very strong odour. That changes in the blood state go with changes in consciousness is exceedingly probable, and would form a fruitful line of study for those who are competent to undertake the investigation. It is noteworthy in this connection that if the trance be unduly prolonged there will be cramp, and even convulsions resembling tetanus, which points to a poisoned blood stream.

The Mental Phenomena of Trance

While the physical phenomena described in the previous chapter are proceeding, a regular series of changes is taking place in consciousness, which we will now consider in their proper sequence.

First comes the relaxation and abstraction of consciousness from mundane things; all thought slows down to a stop even as a flywheel slows down when an engine is to be reversed; then it starts off again focused upon subjective things. It is in order to secure this cessation of conscious thought that it is necessary to have quietness and darkness while the medium is going into trance, The part played by light is very curious, for a trance medium is sensitive to light, not only upon the eyes, but on the whole surface of the skin, especially the back of the head and nape of the neck. It is probable that this sensitiveness would be found to extend down the spine were it not protected by the clothes.

As soon as the necessary slowing down of objective

consciousness has taken place, the subjective consciousness increases greatly in vividness, the images in the imagination becoming extraordinarily clear-cut and intense; nevertheless, they are recognisable as being the products of the image making faculty because they can be changed at will, which is not the case with the images evoked by objective psychic consciousness.

Now comes the dividing of the ways. Up to this point the different types of trance are identical. In each one the shutting down of brain consciousness has taken place. Now begins the opening up of the higher consciousness.

In the case of the Trance of Projection, no attempt is made to keep open the line of communication with the physical brain; the more complete the withdrawal (that is to say, the deeper the trance) the more satisfactory the results.

We will not attempt the study of the Trance of Projection in these pages, however, for it involves so many problems of the deeper aspects of occultism that without a working knowledge of esoteric science its discussion would be unprofitable.

The study of the Trance of Vision we must also reluctantly put aside, for it would lead us too far afield into psychology both orthodox and esoteric. We will therefore limit ourselves to the study of our subject proper, the psychology of trance mediumship; the other types of trance having only been referred to for the purpose of classification.

If the experimenter having thrown himself into a trance, proposes neither to project his subtle self nor to make use of psychic vision, a third course is open to him, and we will explain exactly what takes place under such circumstances, in order that we may have the necessary data available for our consideration.

The experienced medium will have certain spirit controls with whom he is accustomed to get into touch, and it is at this point that he begins the invocation of his control. Soon the answering voice formulates itself in consciousness and a mental conversation is exchanged between the two.

If it is intended to establish communication between the two planes of existence, and the spirit control desires to communicate with the circle who are sitting with the medium, the consciousness of the medium has, as it were, to "put the communicator through."

The control utters some phrase which the medium hears mentally, and instructs the medium to repeat it aloud. In order to do this, the medium has to re-establish contact with his own body. This is a somewhat intricate process.

As soon as the swoop into space takes place, which is recognised as the sensation caused by the ego withdrawing from the physical body, the kinaesthetic sense, which indicates the position of the body in space, undergoes a change, so that, although the position of the body upon the couch remains unaltered, the kinaesthetic sense reports that one is standing upright.

It will thus be perceived that the medium is now upon the same plane as the spirit communicator, he too has shed his body, though in his case but temporarily. In order to carry out the control's instructions and repeat to the earth plane the message given him, usually some brief and simple formula of greeting, the medium proceeds to take control of his own body in just the same way as a spirit communicator does. That is to say, he does not re-enter it, sinking in through the solar plexus till subtle and dense body blend limb by limb as he does when he returns at the end of a trance, but merely contacts the throat centres by projecting his will upon them and, as it were, giving suggestion to them.

With considerable effort the muscles of the larynx are manipulated, though not through their usual channels; the words are spoken, some one in the circle answers, and immediately communication is established. As soon as someone on the physical plane responds, it seems as if the mind of the communicating entity immediately takes over the control of the throat centres of the entranced body, and the medium steps aside. The whole process takes place so swiftly that it is exceedingly difficult to know exactly what happens, but the vital point seems to lie in the reply of some member of the circle. What subtle interaction of mind upon mind takes place is difficult to define. Probably the minds of the sitters are directed towards the personality of the communicator, and thus a rapport is set up. But why, and wherefore, I cannot say. Subsequent communicators, who take over from the first speaker, have no such difficulty in establishing communication.

Communication once established, the body of the medium appears to be used as a telephone by the communicators from another plane of existence. Control and medium seem to have changed places; the medium is now standing aside, and it is the mind of the control that is manipulating the brain and nervous system. The medium is fully conscious, there is no such thing as loss of consciousness in trance; it is only the memory which is frequently obliterated, like the memory of a dream. Nothing but the most intense concentration can keep the medium from involuntarily slipping back into his body. A single thought concerning the earth plane, and he is back. All the time he has to think of himself as being on the inner planes, and disembodied; but so habitually do we think of ourselves as embodied and in terms of our physical sensations, that only a mind that is highly trained in concentration can inhibit these customary thoughts. For this reason an arduous apprenticeship in concentration and mind control is necessary before any one who is not a natural trance medium can throw themselves into trance. In the natural trance medium the dissociation of consciousness takes place automatically and involuntarily, and the processes are so swift as to defy analysis. In the case, however, of a person who has deliberately set himself to acquire the power to go into trance, gradually perfecting his technique as experience grows, it is possible to observe the stages through which consciousness passes, because in the earlier days of his training he painfully and laboriously struggles from one plane to another with intense effort, frequently losing his grip on his mind and sliding back to a lower state of consciousness and from there working his way up again. With experience comes expertness, and the trained occultist will be as "slick" in his transition through the planes of consciousness as the natural psychic.

Trance and Hypnosis

The physical and mental data of trance being now available for consideration, what shall we say concerning the whole matter? Can any one who is familiar with the two sets of phenomena deny that it is a process of auto-hypnosis? But when we have said that, have we said all? Does the adept, highly trained in occult science, who by constant practice has attained skill in throwing himself into trance, achieve results which exceed those obtained by the hypnotist who works on a purely psychological basis?

The answer to this question will surprise many people, both in the ranks of the psychologists and the psychics. The hypnotists have frequently achieved the same results as the occultists. Mesmer himself was in touch with the occultists of his day, but whether he discovered his powers spontaneously and developed and elaborated his system with the help of those who were familiar with the traditional methods of using these little known powers of the mind, or whether he first learnt of them from his illuminist friends and then developed the application of them to the healing of diseases, is not known.

Dr Albert Moll, in his book on hypnotism, which is one of the standard works on the subject, chronicles a list of phenomena which is the envy of the occultist.

Being familiar with both sets of phenomena, I have no hesitation whatsoever in giving it as my opinion that the deliberately induced trance of the adept occultist is a process of auto-hypnosis, and that the intricate rituals of ceremonial magic and initiation ceremonies that have come down from the ancients, or have been elaborated today upon traditional principles, are based upon a knowledge of those little known powers of the mind which today we call hypnosis, auto-suggestion and psycho-analysis. The ancients were aware of these powers, and developed their application to the spiritual unfolding of man just as today we are developing their application to therapeutics.

Occultism and psychotherapy rest on the same basis. There are certain aspects of the mind which are beginning to be understood in the West today and which were well understood by the ancients and in the East. Anyone who investigates the mind impartially, and who is not limited by preconceived concepts, will soon find that he is opening up aspects of consciousness of which he had never hitherto suspected the existence. But the mind being exceedingly subject to suggestion when functioning in these subjective states, it follows that if the investigator contemptuously rejects the first manifestations of supernormal consciousness, those states will immediately close down and the mind limit itself to what is expected of it. If, on the other hand, the investigator is looking for the supernormal states, he will not be long before he finds them. They can be inhibited or brought forth by the clearly held idea in the mind of the investigator.

Let us grant that trance and auto-hypnosis are one and the same thing, and that the hypnotist by means of suggestion can obtain from his subject the same results that the trance medium exhibits spontaneously; in what, then, can we differentiate between hypnosis and trance? It differentiates in this, that in one case there is a visible hypnotist, and in the other there is not. We say visible advisedly, for is it possible that there is an invisible hypnotist?

Here we are opening up a big field of speculation. Who, or what is it, that in the case of self-induced trance, takes the place of the hypnotist, and gives suggestion to the passive subconsciousness? How are we to differentiate auto-suggestion from auto-hypnosis? How are we to tell the difference between a spirit control and a secondary personality, a form of psychopathology with which psychology is well acquainted, and whose mechanisms it can demonstrate?

Up to a point the psychological process appears to be identical in hypnosis, trance, and dissociation of the personality, for in each case the Ego appears to be separated from the personality. An understanding of esoteric science enables us to see how this separation takes place, for according to its doctrines, at each incarnation the individuality, or higher self, which is immortal, builds up a personality, or lower self, consisting of the concrete mind, the emotions and passions, and the physical body with its etheric counterpart of electromagnetic stresses. There is a natural line of cleavage, therefore, between the individuality and personality. If the higher self be in abeyance, the lower self, which is simply a very elaborately organised system of reflexes and associated ideas, is left without a directing intelligence, and will remain passive until stimulated from without, in which case the appropriate complex, or organised system of ideas, will be galvanised into activity, and run through its reaction-circuit till it comes to a stop.

A personality in this condition may be likened to a car standing at the roadside with the engine just ticking over; the owner may get into it, open the throttle, engage the gears, and drive off; or, on the other hand, someone to whom he lends the car may do the same thing, returning the car in due course to its original owner.

It appears as if the elaborate system of inherited reactions and acquired memories that we call the personality of the incarnation is simply a vehicle of consciousness, and is no more the real self than the car is the driver. We habitually identify ourselves with it, because where our consciousness is limited to the brain, we are aware of no other kind of existence; but the trained occultist, knowing that consciousness in reality is not limited by the brain but built the brain as its instrument, is able to escape from the suggestion of the physical senses and know himself as he really is - a spiritual being who has built up out of experience certain instruments of consciousness which serve but limit him. Man is a tool-using animal even on the spiritual plane. Under certain conditions the ego can be separated from its tools, even in life, and then apparently other egos can pick up those tools and use them.

There appear to be two processes in what is usually classified under the one heading as suggestion - either the suggestion is given to the conscious mind, is assimilated by the ego, and then conveyed by it to the subconsciousness. Or the suggestion is given direct to the subconscious mind, the ego being out of the picture for the time being.

Subconsciousness might very well be defined as mind minus ego. It possesses all the characteristics of mind save intelligent direction which can adapt itself to circumstances and serve the general aims of the self. Its different complexes are like mechanical toys which are wound up and run through their tricks till the power of the spring is spent and they come to a stop. They are purposive but not intelligent.

Take away the ego from the personality, and it is simply a collection of co-ordinated motor complexes directed by associated ideas. The only controller is memory. That which has been done before can be done again because the associated idea links are there and evoke each other in their accustomed sequences, but nothing can be originated or adapted. The personality, deprived of the ensouling spiritual intelligence, is nothing but a collection of mechanical toys, that is to say, an automaton. It is this automaton condition that characterises trance and hypnosis.

Now supposing the machine, perfect in all its parts but deserted by its driver, feels another hand on the controls, what then? This, we may presume, is what takes place in hypnosis and spirit control. There is no difference in principle between the control of a hypnotic subject by the mind of the hypnotist, and the control of the entranced medium by the mind of the disembodied spirit. It is a well known and frequently repeated experiment of hypnosis that a good subject can be controlled by the unspoken thought of the hypnotist; there is no difference in kind between the telepathic control exercised by an embodied mind and the telepathic control exercised by a disembodied mind.

Those, of course, who do not believe in the survival of bodily death will be reduced to explaining all trance phenomena by a hypothesis which excludes this possibility, but in the face of the accumulated evidence of psychic research, one may not unjustifiably describe them as the die-hards of materialistic science. Those who are prepared to concede the possibility of the survival of bodily death by some form of integrated consciousness cannot logically exclude the possibility of telepathic operations by that consciousness.

If it be conceded that there is sufficient evidence available to justify the opinion that under certain circumstances, e.g. under hypnosis and in trance, the Ego is cut off from the personality, so that the personality is deprived of intelligent direction, and can be manipulated by the mind of another, and if it be further conceded that organised consciousness can survive bodily death, there seems no reason to deny the possibility of spirit communication through a trance medium, for in cases that we are able to examine experimentally we can see the same modus operandi.

It is difficult to see how, in the face of the accumulated evidence, either of these hypotheses can be denied; and if they are admitted, their implication follows naturally, and we have an explanation of the nature of trance mediumship which links it on to the known and proven facts of hypnosis, suggestion, and telepathy.

The Technique of Trance

Having arrived thus far, our next consideration must be concerning the exact nature of the process by means of which the separation between the ego and the personality is effected.

Let us first consider the normal process of the mind; it consists of a ceaseless streaming of images across the illuminated screen of consciousness. It may best be likened to the projection of a movie. It does not appear to be possible for two trains of ideas to occupy the focus of consciousness simultaneously, but the alternation can be so rapid that to a superficial observer they appear to be superimposed. This ceaseless succession of ideas appears to be of the very essence of the nature of consciousness.

We can get an interesting insight into this matter if we study themental exercises performed by the occultist when he is engaged in acquiring the faculty of going into trance. These mental exercises have been handed down in the Mystery Schools from time immemorial, and are even better known and more highly developed in the East than they are in the West. They can be found in many books on mind training, notably in those emanating from mystical and occult circles. The comparative study of these, and the different yoga systems, soon suffices to show that they are all founded on the same principles.

The earlier exercises are directed to teaching the pupil to follow a train of thought without mind wandering. He has, in fact, to learn to inhibit unwanted thoughts as the first essential of his training. He soon acquires considerable proficiency in this, and a good student can follow a train of thought for a considerable length of time without any obtruding ideas arising, becoming quite oblivious of his surroundings. The story of Newton working out mathematical formulae with his papers on fire could be told of many an occult student.

The power to follow a definite train of thought is succeeded by exercises designed to teach the student to concentrate on a single thought and perceive in it all its implications without allowing the mind to move from it. In this case the mind is circling round a fixed centre instead of proceeding forward in a straight line.

This process differs markedly from the preceding one in that ideas are not sought, but, alien images being inhibited, are allowed to *rise* into consciousness. There is a great difference between directive thinking and allowing ideas to rise. It is one of the points in esoteric psychology that have important practical applications. The use of this method of mentation is a knack which is hard to describe; its acquirement often resists the utmost efforts of the student until he realises that his effort has to be directed to inhibiting, not originating, whereupon he may suddenly acquire the trick.

Once acquired, it is comparatively easy to practise, and renders available the riches of the subconscious mind, thus bringing a tremendous increase to the scope and power of the personality. This method is used in psychoanalysis, but its applications have been brought to a far higher degree of specialisation by the occultist, who makes much use of them in the course of his work. It is a form of mentation notably characteristic of genius, and accounts for the rapid and effortless nature of the highest types of creative art.

The final stage in the training for trance consists in the practice of formulating a mental picture of some simple form such as a black circle on a white ground, and visualising it mentally and holding it steadily before the mind's eye for considerable periods. The first attempts at such an exercise yield some rather interesting results and throw a good deal of light upon the nature of thought. It is easy enough to formulate the image, but very difficult to make it hold still. It will dance about, swing like a pendulum, go far off and approach again, do anything, in fact, except stay put. One of the modifications of this exceedingly difficult exercise, by means of which it is approached step by step, consists in formulating the image, and then watching it swing at the end of a pendulum. Or again, the image may be seen as stationary, with the background moving behind it, like landscape sliding past a train window. Either of these devices aids greatly in enabling the image to be held before consciousness; but stand still for any length of time it will not, as any one can prove for themselves by trying the experiment. This experience bears out the statement that thought is like a cine-film, a constant succession of images, and that to hold it still is to stop the show.

But let us consider our study of the last yoga exercise. When expertness is obtained, it becomes possible to hold the image still for considerable lengths of time, but it will be found that as soon as the image is stilled, consciousness of external impressions is lost and time passes unheeded. A few minutes may seem like long periods of time, or, contrarily, several hours may pass without any apparent break in the continuity of consciousness.

Is there any difference between the voluntary stilling of the thought processes by fixing the mind's eye upon some imagined object, and that of fixing the physical eyes on some bright object? Both methods tend to slow thought to a standstill and to break the sequence of the unceasing stream of mental images, leaving the broken ends in mid-air. In order to go into trance or under hypnosis, the conscious mind is literally jammed, as if one had poked a stick into its wheels, and so brought it to a standstill.

When the constant stream of images ceases to pass through the mind, it seems as if the Ego were no longer bound to the body. It is a maxim of esoteric science that where the attention is directed, there is the soul present. As long as the attention of consciousness is directed towards the sensations derived from the body, the soul, to put it crudely, is in the body; but as soon as attention is cut off from the body, the soul is no longer bound to it, but is free upon its own plane. The difficulty lies in withdrawing all attention from the body, for concentration upon the symbol has to be so complete that no physical sensation is felt, not even the kinaesthetic sense, which tells us the position of the limbs in space. Only very great powers of concentration can achieve this, and therefore the trained trance medium who can go into deep trance is rare.

So great is the concentration achieved by the trained occultist that it has been known successfully to mask the pain of severe scalds and permit of sleep without the use of drugs.

The unconsciousness of trance differs from that of anaesthesia, syncope, or concussion in that the separation between the higher and lower aspects of consciousness takes place at a different level. In anaesthesia and other forms of what we will denominate physical unconsciousness, it is the physical vehicle of consciousness that is put out of commission so that the Ego cannot make use of it. The separation then, is between the physical body and the personality, not between the personality and the individuality, or higher self. In sleep the separation seems to take place between the lower and higher aspects of the personality, so that a certain amount of the personality and its consciousness remains with the physical body. Thus the higher self is still bound to matter, because the higher aspects of the personality are associated with it and therefore in ordinary sleep it is not free to function on its own plane. Thus the three types of living unconsciousness - physical unconsciousness, sleep, and trance, are differentiated by the difference in plane of the point at which the higher self with its self consciousness separates from the lower self, which is built up by the experience during incarnation, and consists of organised systems of cognitive complexes.

Our study of trance would be incomplete unless we considered the way in which the medium gets into touch with the communicating entity. To the consciousness of the medium, now withdrawn from the body, the communicating entity appears as a very clear-cut picture seen with the mind's eye. He visualises the mentality which he feels trying to contact his own. As soon as he is able to form a clear mental picture of it, the dim sense of a presence gives place to the formulation of words heard mentally; he gets a distinct sense of a definite personality, and the sitters who form his circle, if they are accustomed to receive communications from a group of controls with whom they have become familiar, will also get a sense of a personality being present, and if they are experienced, will be able to recognise which control it is before any communication comes through. This is strong evidence in favour of the objectivity of spirit controls as against the theory that they are secondary personalities of the medium's own self, dissociated according to the well known laws of psychopathology, such as have been studied in detail by Dr Morton Prince and others.

Now it is obvious that the medium cannot really be seeing anything, because the corporeal form of the communicating entity has long since mouldered to dust, so that if he saw the actual physical form of the entity, it would appear as a skeleton wrapped in shreds of grave clothes. But instead of this he sees the communicator as he or she appeared in life. It is obvious, therefore, that what he is seeing is the entity's mental picture of itself, communicated to him telepathically. It is the same mechanism which is employed if two living people are trying to communicate telepathically. The transmitter visualises as clearly as he can the person with whom he wishes to communicate and then imagines himself as speaking to him. The receiver, if he is at all sensitive, will frequently have a clear mental picture of the communicator and hear the words he speaks.

We may reasonably conclude, therefore, that what takes place between two embodied minds when they try to communicate telepathically also takes place between an embodied and a disembodied mind when they try to communicate telepathically.

The communicating entity visualises himself as he was when in the body; the medium is able to perceive this thought form psychically, and it forms the means of communication between them. Once this contact has been established, the medium is able to get into psychic touch with any spirit control whom he knows by visualising him. It has also been found that, by employing the same device, mediums can invoke each other's control.

We may therefore disabuse our minds of the idea that "control" is the same thing as "obsession" as popularly understood; that is to say, that the body of one person is occupied by the soul of another. What we are dealing with in trance mediumship is the hypnotic influence of the mind of the disembodied spirit over the mind of the medium, and it will be found that the whole of the phenomena of trance mediumship can be explained in terms of the psychology of hypnosis.

This explanation is in no wise meant to discredit trance mediumship, but to explain it and even to extend its scope and make it more readily accessible. The knowledge of hypnosis was one of the most carefully guarded secrets of the ancient Mysteries, and if we recognise the principles of hypnosis, telepathy, and the survival of bodily death by intelligent consciousness, we have the key to three words which turns the lock of trance mediumship.

All occult schools depend for their working on their contacts with those who are known to them as the Masters. Different schools are in touch with different Masters, and it is the portraits, names, or symbols of these Masters which are among their most carefully guarded secrets. Of course the Masters are nothing more nor less than spirit controls of a high type.

Those who are familiar with occult literature will have realised that the presence we have described is what is known to occultists as the Master, to mystics as the vision of a saint, to spiritualists as the control, and is repeatedly described in the Bible as the visit of an angel, such an one as taught the interpretations of dreams to the prophet Daniel and announced to the Virgin Mary her destiny.

It is noteworthy that the spiritualist, the occultist, the mystic, the prophet, and the seer all bear witness to such meetings with invisible visitants from another plane of existence.

Such divergent witnesses giving corroborative evidence establishes it as certain that some common experience must be at the bottom of it. The fact that the lunatic adds his testimony to the cloud of witnesses need not necessarily invalidate the evidence, for it may be that the experiences of those possessed of superconsciousness may throw light on the hallucinations of the lunatic, instead of vice versa. At any rate, the source whence Daniel drew his power to impress two successive kings of Babylon and Joan of Arc drew her influence over a king of France and his generals, cannot be dismissed as such stuff as dreams are made of unless we are prepared to admit that the stuff is real in its own sphere.

To say that a thing is imaginary is not to dispose of it in the realm of mind, for the imagination, or image making faculty, is a very important part of our mental functioning. An image formed by the imagination is a reality from the point of view of psychology; it is quite true that it has no physical existence, but are we going to limit reality to that which is material? We shall be far out of our reckoning if we do, for mental images are potent things, and although they do not actually exist on the physical plane, they influence it far more than most people suspect.

COMMENTARY

We have seen in the Commentary to Part One how Dion Fortune made some splash about her mediumistic powers and methods during 1942. We know from the archives that she had been using this technique since at least 1921. However, there was always a certain ambivalence about it, and in 1930 we find her writing up some of her own conclusions with regard to trance mediumship. She was obviously aware that although she was getting what she regarded as good results from it, it was by no means a technique that was looked upon favourably by other occult teachers. Thus in the July 1930 issue of "The Inner Light" she devoted an article to it.

The Problem of Trance

The problem of trance is a vexed one in occult circles. Some schools, and among these are the most widely known, condemn its use unsparingly. They say that in trance the soul is in a passive state, and to be in a passive state on the Inner Planes is to invite obsession. Such a sweeping condemnation shows that there has been no practical experience of trance, otherwise it would be known that there is more than one kind of trance, and the objections that may justly apply to one have no bearing on another, nor is passivity, under certain conditions, either dangerous or even harmful.

There are only two kinds of trance which can justly be called passive, the trance into which the hypnotist throws his subject, and the trance into which a certain type of psychic falls spontaneously. The other two types, which we will call the Trance of Vision and the Trance of Projection, are intensely active, with full consciousness and control on the Inner Planes.

Hypnotic trance is induced by very powerful suggestion

reinforced by psychic manipulation of the etheric double, so that consciousness is, as it were, thrown out of gear. The physical and etheric bodies are pushed slightly out of alignment by the manipulations of the etheric forces by the hypnotist. It is for this reason that suggestion, and suggestion alone, (that is to say, purely mental manipulation) is insufficient to induce deep trance. The hypnotist has to have the power, natural or acquired, of operating etherically and manipulating the etheric double of his subject. It is not everybody that has this power, and therefore it is not everybody that can hypnotise. If the hypnotist is incompetent, malicious, or employing an undesirable method, he can, of course, do as much damage to his patient as a bad surgeon. The hypnotic trance is a drastic surgery of the mind. For this reason it is very seldom used, most operators preferring to rely upon a light hypnosis, in which the patient is merely drowsy and abstracted, fully conscious, but lulled and dreamy. This is all that is required for any manipulations of the mind that are to be performed for the benefit of the patient. Deep, cataleptic trance is only induced in the course of research work. It does no harm in the hands of a skilful operator, but it is not a thing to be played with, and certainly not a thing to undergo frequently.

The uninitiated psychic who goes into spontaneous trance is a person whose consciousness tends to "slip its gears". This slipping of the gears of consciousness ranges from absentmindedness to catalepsy. In both hypnosis and psychic trance the soul of the subject is merely thrown out of alignment with the centres in the physical body which are the points of contact of consciousness. Consequently the body is passive, possibly rigid, because the flexor and extensor muscles are no longer co-ordinated, and may both contract simultaneously, thereby immobilising each other.

In such cases the mind itself is passive; it is that dreamy state we observe in a person under light hypnosis. Any other mind, whether incarnate or discarnate, which comes into touch with it, finds it hyper-suggestible. In this state, anything may happen, and it only needs some slight knowledge of the denizens of the astral plane to suggest possibilities of unpleasantness.

It is a person with this peculiar psychic constitution who, when developed, becomes the trance medium with which we are familiar in spiritualistic circles. The work is not without its risks, but we shall achieve nothing outstanding in any walk of life unless we are prepared to take risks, and in experienced and trustworthy hands, the risks of trance mediumship are not undue.

If the leader of the circle is skilled and conscientious, he will be able to take his medium in and out of this state without permitting any untoward happenings to occur, and such an operation has its uses in the field of psychic experimentation. It is not therefore to be decried unreservedly; neither, on the other hand, is it to be recommended save for research experiments in the hands of an experienced operator who is able to command suitable conditions, the subject being a person of normal mentality in sound health, with an intellectual appreciation of the metaphysics of the work in hand.

The drawback to such experiences, from the point of view of the subject, is a tendency to permanently increased suggestibility, and a liability to get into a habit of falling into trance on slight provocation. Therefore experiments should be few and far between, allowing ample time for a return to normality between each one; half a dozen experiments is the limit in one series, and some months should elapse between series. But with such precautions, and the proper sealing of the room in which the work is done, there is no undue risk in the work, and I for one, refuse to join in the parrot cry against such experiments. I see no reason why people with the requisite qualifications should not undertake them and enrich our knowledge by their results.

The true occult trance, the temple sleep of the adept, is in quite a different category from the types previously considered. The initiate who, by his knowledge of the necessary technique, throws himself deliberately into trance is no more passive than the diver swimming under water. It is only by the most strenuous activity, that a swimmer can overcome the natural buoyancy of his body and descend to any depth. So it is with the mind. It is only by concentrated effort that we can hold the mind to superconsciousness; as soon as the effort is relaxed, it will return to normal. Trance merges in sleep, and vision gives place to dream.

It is this tendency of trance to merge in sleep which is the principal difficulty with which the occultist has to contend. There are two weak spots in his defences, which we will call the cusps of sleep. The transition from waking consciousness to sleep, and from sleep to psychic consciousness is always through a psychic "dead centre". A wheel, which is reversing its revolution, has to stop for a second, however brief. When consciousness is passing from objective to subjective, and then out to objective again, the mind has to become a complete blank, all associated trains of thought have to be broken, and a completely fresh start made in the new mode. The person who goes into either the hypnotic or the mediumistic trance gets as far as this dead centre and then stops there until pushed out of it by an external force, usually the will of another, whether that other be the incarnate hypnotist or a discarnate spirit. The technique of the occultist teaches him to swing himself over this dead centre by means of an association of ideas which stretches out like a bridge-head across the abyss, so that he has only to make a comparatively small spring in order to alight on the far shore.

The bridge-head thus projected out into the Unseen starts as pictorial imagination and passes gradually into the Trance of Vision. When this occurs attention is withdrawn from the objective world, and therefore to all intents and purposes, the experimenter is unconscious, though he can be roused without much difficulty. He is not out of his body and functioning on the Astral Plane, but is looking into it as through a periscope.

In the Trance of Projection, however, the Body of Light is formulated on the Astral, and consciousness projected into it. The physical body is then in a truly cataleptic condition, all consciousness being withdrawn.

We shall get much light on our subject if we observe what happens to the beginner in occultism who is striving to master the technique of trance. He will achieve with comparative readiness the Trance of Vision, for as soon as attention is withdrawn from the physical plane, the astral plane of picture consciousness opens up. He has only to acquire sufficient power of concentration to be able to turn attention away from the physical sensation for the phantasmagoria of the subjective sphere to commence passing before his mental sight. Of course it is one thing to look into the kaleidoscope of the astral, and another to pick out and follow any desired thread of vision, but that consideration we cannot enter upon now.

Unless, however, by a deliberate effort of will, the connection with brain consciousness be maintained by either speaking aloud or writing down that which is passing across the inner sight, the Trance of Vision will speedily change into the Trance of Projection, and the experimenter will find that he has apparently left his body and is actually in the midst of his vision and taking part in it, instead of seeing it as a series of mental pictures. He will have slid into a deeper trance than he meant to, and will have his work cut out to scramble ashore again.

Any experienced occult teacher will tell him that he must on no account experiment with the Trance of Projection until he has mastered the technique of the Trance of Vision so that he can follow a train of vision images through the tangled subjective jungle with a great degree of certitude, and is able to turn round and come back along the memory trail should he lose the thread of his vision; for it is upon this power to retrace a memory trail that he will depend for his safe return to his body after he has been out in the Trance of Projection; in other words, he depends upon his power to follow a single line of thought without any distraction for the linking up of the levels of consciousness after he has dissociated them. If he fails to maintain the sequence of consciousness, he will develop schizophrenia, or personality splitting. This will be found to be the explanation of the peculiarities of character and conduct that we not infrequently observe among those who go in for practical occultism.

Let us continue, however, to follow the career of the student of occultism who is learning to go into trance. After a certain amount of experience he will have reached the point when he will be able readily to close down objective consciousness and obtain a clear focus of the inner vision. At first he will find the subjective pictures will be merely an elaboration of what the psychologist calls hypnogogics - those small, bright, clear cut pictures which sometimes rise in the mind as sleep encroaches upon consciousness, and also, though more rarely, in moments of abstraction. He will have developed expertness in focussing these and holding them steady, one at a time, before the inner vision, and giving an account of them.

Then, one day in front of this magic mirror of his vision will step something which is a reality among all the shadows. The experimenter has hitherto been perceiving thought forms in the racial subconsciousness; what he sees now, although it has the same appearance as the rest, is a reality, and he instinctively knows it to be such because he feels it to be ensouled, for deep calls to deep, and the spark of divine spirit within himself reacts to the spark of divine spirit within the appearance that presents itself to his inner sight. To describe it more clearly than that is impossible, but just as even a child will know death from sleep, so the seer, when he perceives that which has life behind it, ought to be able to distinguish it from the swarming pictures which are but after images left upon the retina of the planet. But though he may know theoretically of the existence of such beings as we are describing, if he has never actually met one, he may mistake unusually vivid picture images for such an encounter, but if he has once seen the reality, he will be very unlikely to make that mistake again, because he will find that the real presence has an effect on him which is never equalled by the vision pictures. It is the difference between seeing a man killed on a film and a man killed in the street.

The initiated occultist has methods of recognising these presences, and finding out who they are and what they are, but there is nothing except experience which will tell the uninitiated experimenter whether he is dealing with a reality or not, and that is where many psychic experiments go wrong.

What, however is it that the experimenter has perceived as a reality amongst dream images? The occultist replies that it is one of three things; it may be the subtle form of another occultist functioning in the Trance of Projection, it may be the earth-bound soul of a dead person, which for certain reasons into which we need not enter now has not yet drawn clear of the material plane; or, finally, it may be the appearance presented by one of those souls of a higher development than the average of humanity which, in the Eastern expression, has won freedom from the wheel of birth and death, having nothing further to learn from the experiences of embodiment in matter.

If the encounter be with either of the two former types of entity, the experimenter will usually be able to maintain his contact with his physical environment and report that which he sees, deliver messages, or allow automatic writing to take place. We therefore need not consider these two forms of the astral encounter any further, for they fall outside our subject, as has already been noted.

Should, however, the encounter be with the third type of entity, the matter is on a different plane altogether. The effect of such an encounter, except in the case of a very experienced occultist, is so to grip the attention and overmaster the mind of the experimenter, that the Trance of Vision immediately changes into the Trance of Projection, and he finds himself withdrawn from the body and face to face with his visitor on its own plane of existence. What is experienced then depends upon the nature of both visitant and experimenter, and is beyond the scope or our present consideration.

Despite the air of revelation in which Dion Fortune announced her own practice of trance mediumship in 1942, it would appear to have been at least a very open "secret" in the immediately pre-war years. In "The Inner Light" magazine for April 1938, she revealed a close acquaintance with the processes of mediumship plainly from her personal experience.

What she has to say is an important contribution to the literature of the subject, for she was a trained rather than a natural medium, it would seem at the hands of her first occult teacher, one of the old school, Dr. Theodore Moriarty, who served as a model for her fictional hero Dr. Taverner. Moreover she had a background of first hand psychotherapeutic experience and psychological knowledge buttressed by her marriage to a medical practitioner. Also her teacher in the Hermetic Order of the Golden Dawn, Maia Curtis-Webb, (later Tranchell-Hayes) was the wife of a leading psychiatrist.

Here is what she had to say in 1938.

How Trance Communication is Made

Those who have some acquaintance with the inner workings of the Fraternity of the Inner Light know that it possesses a quantity of teachings that have been received psychically and that are referred to generically as "The Words of the Masters." These have been published in part in the pages of "The Inner Light" magazine, are read aloud at some of the meetings, and are used as the basis of certain of the inner group teaching. Persons who have had access to these MSS. say that they have a very marked effect upon the consciousness of those who read them - an effect out of all proportion to their intrinsic content.

These communications were received by means of trance mediumship, myself acting as the medium and various Masters who are behind the Order which is behind the Fraternity acting as controls.

We must therefore, in order to make our explanation comprehensive, examine the manner in which this transmission took place.

Mediumship consists in the power to disconnect the rational mind from the subconscious mind, leaving the latter swinging freely, like a compass needle. The subconscious mind, which is normally capable of perceiving thoughts and influences psychically with varying degrees of clarity - being, in fact, the seat of the psychic faculties - can be influenced by means of telepathic suggestion. If telepathy is a fact, and survival is a fact, and the evidence in favour of both these things is very considerable, there is no more inherent difficulty in telepathy being performed by a discarnate mind than by an incarnate one since the physical brain is in no case the instrument that is used.

Occultists traditionally decry trance mediumship, saying that it is the wrong method of development, and so it is as a general routine practice in a training school, whose aim should be to make all its students competent psychics rather than to depend upon the specially developed powers of one or two mediums among them. It should also be remembered that the person who is used as a medium gets nothing out of the communications save an hour or two's sound sleep. Nevertheless, all actively working schools of which I have any knowledge have made use of mediumship in their establishment at least, and their energy fades when there is no "school of prophets" among them; it seems as if this direct means of transmission between the planes puts life into a school as nothing else does. When it ceases, the fire dies down in the furnace that provides the driving power of the Fraternity. When the lines of communication are open and being actively used, there is a big head of steam in the boiler of that particular organisation.

All occult organisations, however, have a rhythm, being alternately active in the Inner and in the Outer. The more intense the activity, the more marked is the periodicity. This rhythm is, of course, really the rhythm of the leader of the group, who is responsible for maintaining the inner plane contacts. There are times when one turns in, as it were, becoming withdrawn from the outer world; taking little part in the active work of the organisation and leaving it to be carried on by lieutenants. Even one's personality appears to shrink in significance as the Higher Self is withdrawn and turned inward. The organisation has then to run with its own momentum, and if it has a truly impersonal system of organisation, it is able to do this. It will, however, gradually lose its impetus, and if no fresh impulse comes to carry it on to further heights, it will slow up and come to a standstill.

Occult organisations have to be continually revivified by fresh impulses of inspiration if they are to maintain their vitality. Some among their leading members must be able to withdraw periodically onto the inner planes to return revivified, bringing with them their sheaves. The keeping open of these lines of contact with the inner planes is all-important, and there must be a constant come and go between this world and the next if the vitality of a Fraternity is to be maintained. Trance mediumship therefore has its part in occult work, for it is by means of trance that those who are in the body are able to free themselves from it temporarily, and those who have not got bodies, (i.e. the Masters) are able to avail themselves of a body temporarily. It must not be thought from this that in an occult fraternity trance mediumship is taught as part of the system. It is not, for there is the well tried occult tradition that every man should be his own medium and not be dependent upon the powers of another for his spiritual contacts. But we understand the technique of trance mediumship and make use of it as required, thus bringing an influx of energy into an organisation which can be obtained in no other way, for much more comes through in trance mediumship than the spoken word, and when a Master is the control a tremendous amount of psychic force is received, not only by those who are present and hear the actual words, but by the group mind of the whole organisation.

Some explanation of the psychology of mediumship will be useful in enabling us to understand the nature of these communications and assess them at their true worth, being neither superstitious nor unduly sceptical. I will therefore give the explanation that was given me, together with such psychological comment and explanation as shall make it more easily understandable. As an ounce of experience is worth a pound of theory, I will speak of my own experience when acting as medium.

The person who is to act as medium picks up the contact of the Masters psychically, either by "calling up" a particular Master, as it were, or by being "called up" by a Master wishing to communicate. At the appointed time a curious sense of power begins to gather, as if one were waiting for a race to start, and those present who are familiar with the procedure can generally recognise who the communicator is going to be.

Whoever is going to act as medium must then open the channel of communication by disconnecting the conscious mind from the subconscious mind and going into trance.

The first stage in this operation consists in completely relaxing every muscle of the body; a dim light is necessary, and relative quiet. Light, in my experience, affects the aura and not merely the eyes, for bandaged eyes and a thick rug are no protection against it. Absence of noise is necessary in order to enter into trance, but once depth of trance is obtained, a reasonable amount of noise is immaterial, with the sole exception of sharp percussive sounds, such as a car back-firing or a chair being knocked over. Light has a far more drastic effect than sound; a shade slipping slightly on a lamp will break a trance that street noises do not affect. That, at any rate, is how it is with me; for although after long experience of the work, I have become fairly immune to noise, I have never attained any degree of immunity to light.

The next stage in the proceedings consists in building up in the imagination a picture of the Master who is going to communicate and concentrating on it. This imaginary picture, as I watch it with the mind's eye, takes on life and absorbs my attention to the exclusion of all else. It is no longer a case of concentrating, though that is the necessary preliminary - it is a case of being held fascinated with the same kind of fascination that one watches a street accident taking place - unable to look away even if one wanted to. All consciousness of my surroundings blots out; there is a curious squinting sensation behind the eyes, which is probably caused by the eyeballs rolling up as they do in deep sleep; then comes another, and none too pleasant sensation as of going down in a fast lift. I seem to lose consciousness for a moment, and then recover it to find myself floating about two feet above my own body, wrapped like a mummy; or sometimes, when the trance has been particularly deep and there is a good deal of power, of standing upright behind my own head, facing the communicator, who stands upright at my feet.

As communication opens there is a period of awkwardness and uncertainty, the attempt to establish communication tending to push me back into my body and break the trance; it is rather like taking an anaesthetic. There is a kind of give and take between my personality and the control, my personality involuntarily trying to struggle back into the body, and my higher consciousness and the control jointly trying to get it out. It reminds me of nothing so much as getting a reluctant horse into a railway van. By this time my focus of consciousness is well established on the inner planes, and I am on the same level of consciousness as the Master who is going to take control, and between us we haul the reluctant personality out more or less forcibly. Once out, it goes to sleep and gives no more trouble, and in its sleep the happenings of the trance are reflected in vague dreams.

I am by now in three pieces. There is the physical body, which has almost stopped breathing and is as good as dead so far as I am concerned, and for all I care; there is the sleeping astral wraith, resembling the traditional ghost, and visible to psychic, though not to physical sight; and there is my own wide awake and active mentality in full possession of its faculties. Associated with the physical body on the couch there is, however, what I conceive to be the subconscious content of memory. It is exactly like a box of many coloured mosaic blocks from which one can build up a picture, and I believe that the communicator is limited by the contents of that box - if a particular colour is not present, he has to manage without it and his picture is incomplete.

The next move, we are told, is for the communicator to build up a mental image of himself and superimpose it upon the passive subconscious personality that remains as a kind of psychological residuum in the physical body, the higher, directive faculties being in abeyance or withdrawn. The whole process can be described in psychological terms as a form of hypnosis, with a discarnate entity as the hypnotist; or it can be described in the traditional psychic and occult terminology; the two are not contradictory or mutually exclusive, but on the contrary throw much light on each other.

The personality thus built up in the subconscious mind that has been deprived of the guidance of its rational self, appears to be the vehicle of communication of the controlling entity. It is, in fact, a "dramatisation" such as the work of the Salpétriere has made us familiar with in the literature of psychopathology, the only difference between my dissociation of personality and that of the unhappy patients at the Salpêtrière being that in my case it remains under my control; I can take my personality apart at will, though I need cooperation from the inner planes if there is to be communication; but, on the other hand, I have never known my personality to come to pieces involuntarily which, of course, is what happened to the Salpêtriere patients. Equally, I can do what those poor souls could not do, and get the component levels of consciousness accurately co-ordinated again after the operation.

This power, to take my personality apart and join it up again, has been perfected by years of practice, after I had been taught the method by my first guru. It always requires considerable effort, but of recent years I have acquired the skill to do it quickly and neatly and without fuss. It can be described as auto-hypnosis or as astral projection according to whether the terminology employed be that of psychology or psychic research.

Re-co-ordination appears to take place in two ways. If there is no "spirit control," and I have shifted the level of consciousness in order to work on the inner planes, I connect up the two levels of consciousness by retracing link by link the association chain of picture images that I used in coming out. Thus, if I used a mental picture of an Egyptian pylon to pass through and go out, I would use the same mental picture to pass through the reverse way when returning. This serves to re-associate consciousness and keep memory intact, and after all, personality is entirely a matter of memory. When, however, there is a control in charge, I go into deep meditation once I have "handed over," and it is his responsibility to see me safely back into my body again. I do not know exactly how this is accomplished; I simply find myself waking up out of deep sleep, feeling very cramped, and with a vague and rapidly fading memory of incoherent dreams. My memory is a very uncertain quantity on these occasions; sometimes I remember a little; sometimes I remember nothing; nevertheless, a residuum seems to remain in the background of the subconsciousness, and sometimes reappears in my writings, or even in conversation, though I am quite unaware of its connection with the trance until I am told of it.

I fairly frequently have the experience on awakening, of finding the kinaesthetic sensation of my feet to be in one place, and my feet themselves in another, with a consequent difficulty in balancing and walking straight when I try to use feet that are not where I expect them to be; and to drop things or knock them over when the same condition prevails in my hands. I was very interested to see in Tschiffelings' account of his famous "Ride," that he had a precisely similar sensation after smoking opium, and went reeling very precariously back to his hotel in consequence. I also see things blurred for a few minutes on first recovering consciousness, and have occasionally seen them double for a second or two.

When once the dazed, drowsy state has worn off I have a sensation of tremendous vitality and energy; I am like a battery that has been re-charged, and this energisation continues for several days and shows itself markedly in my writing, which improves in quality and is greatly increased in output, and also in my power of leadership. I experience a marked increase in driving-force, conceive of all manner of new schemes, and want to get on with them. Far from affecting adversely my energy or mental acuity, I am of the opinion that trance markedly enhances them.

These, then, are the bases on which my work has been built up. I have behind me the training and technique of the Western Esoteric Tradition into which I have been initiated on the physical plane, and I have also direct access to the inner planes.

That her practical work along these lines goes back to early in her occult career is demonstrated in one of the earliest trance records by Dion Fortune that is still extant, which dates from 8th February 1921.

Sitting of 8.2.1921

You are now in contact for information on trance.

Trance is of two kinds: the trance of perception, and the trance of communication.

In the trance of perception the subject closes down the physical sense organs, passes into a subjective state, and then becomes objective upon a higher plane. If the plane of consciousness is to be the mental, the subject remains subjective on the astral and does not become objective until the plane is reached for functioning.

The danger point for all psychic work is the astral. When it is intended to function on the astral, the subject should pass subjectively through the astral state of consciousness and become objective upon the upper mental. Then from the upper mental use the lower mental as a subconscious; pass from the conscious upper mental into a subjective state on the lower mental and thence become objective on the astral. Thus one approaches the astral from above. One comes down in power, and safely. Return in the same way. Always pass the lower astral subjectively, and then one meets nothing worse than one's own complexes.

In the second state, of trance communication, the subject passes subjectively to the appointed level and steps aside, the communicating entity makes contact with the subject's nerve endings, thus assuming control.

This should never be done by the voluntary action of the subject or any member of the circle but should only be effected from the "other side" by the Master in charge, and will seldom be made use of. When it is done, the possessing entity will give you a sign of identity. You will get to know these signs. You can at any time you wish, send a messenger to make an appointment with any entity whose name and sign you may know. Do not do this unless necessary for these are high powers, and while they will aid you in necessity, will not regard kindly an unnecessary invocation. You can conduct all ordinary phases of your research by a sub-method of method two.

The subject goes to the appointed level subjectively, the personality steps aside, the unit of incarnation steps aside and the individuality, the unit of evolution, comes into manifestation. The entity, or individuality, brings with it the knowledge of its past, its power to function upon all planes, its power to direct perception of the secrets of nature, its knowledge of the boding causes, its capacity to act as a channel for the transmission of power. As time goes on and the right conditions, this individuality will function more and more, coming through in full waking consciousness...the perfect synthesis of the whole consciousness which enables the supra-consciousness to manifest. This is the meaning of initiation.

It is necessary that you should understand the methods of entering upon trance. The subject, by withdrawing attention from the phenomenal world, passes into a subjective condition, and then does one of three things:

i) becomes objective upon a higher plane;
ii) steps aside for another entity to speak; or
iii) the individuality comes into manifestation.

Guard well against premature psychism, when the subject, having passed to a subjective condition, constructs a phantasy. This is a great source of confusion in psychism. Emotion on the part of the subject gives rise to this condition. None can pass to the higher levels save those who are desireless, because desire holds the focussing part of the Ego - the point of manifestation - to the level of repressed wishes, and it is these wishes that are expressed in the form of an audible dream, this state being a true somnambulism. Therefore take all communications in the cool light of the morning, and sift them by the test of Freudian symbolism, watching well for the wish fulfilment of the subject's unconscious. This is your source of error. You are also liable to error from lying spirits. Therefore let the "bar" guard, by her knowledge of practical occultism, against the intrusion of the evil ones.

That is her function in this work. There is the terminal that draws down from the higher level. There is the terminal that transmits the manifestation. And there is the "bar" between. You will observe, at the commencement of the work that the subject withdraws from phenomenal consciousness, passes into sleep, thence into trance. You will know when sleep gives place to trance by the sound in the throat as the thyroid closes. You will know when the subject passes into the objective condition by the raising of the hands to call down power. You will know when the subject brings this power through to the circle by the outstretching of the hands. Make contact then, let hand take hand to join the triangle, the male to the left, the female to the right. You will know by the crossing of the hands on the breast, and the sign of the Good Shepherd, that contact has been made with the Master. Then the work can proceed.

If, during the subsequent three days, free association be employed, much additional information can be extracted from the subconscious of the subject, for much more is given than she can bring through.

A somewhat unusual terminology seems to be employed in designating those who were taking part. It would seem that besides the medium, (referred to as *the subject*), two others were physically present. A man acting as scribe and taking down what was said, is referred to as *the terminal*, who draws things down from a higher level. This could not have been her close associate C.T.Loveday, who did not turn up until the next year. There is also a woman with esoteric knowledge present, who is referred to as *the bar -* and acts as a kind of guardian, to guard the integrity of the medium whilst she is in a passive trance state, in this case Maia Curtis-Webb. The inner plane communicator is referred to as *the transmitting terminal,* in this case one apparently of Master rank that she contacted at Glastonbury in the early days of her occult work.

The trance work of the earlier years of Dion Fortune show a certain informal ad hoc approach that is sometimes amusing in retrospect, as for example, the comments of one of the communicators, Carstairs, on 9th December 1922:

"I am in luck this evening. I have come in for the fag end of a piece of candy. When we link up we link with the senses - with the etheric body, that's where we join, it has compensations about Christmas time."

Or on another occasion:

(V.M.F. found asleep.) Instructions given to call group and lower lights.

David: Hello. So you have got yourselves tangled up again. That is because the forces are running so strongly. Carry on. It is merely cramping. I will give you one piece of advice - don't leave her alone when the power tides are about, because if she goes sub-con in a cramped position she will kick till she gets comfortable and the best thing you can do is to straighten her out and tidy her up. You can't get any depth of trance until she is straight.
(Awoke and tidied up.)

Well you have got tidy anyway. If they can get through they will communicate. I am just killing time. You have got too much light. There are two of them want to speak to you if they can get through, but the trance isn't deep enough for them. I always seem to get everybody's leavings.

From these early beginnings it is of interest to track forward to the end of 1944 to find further considerations on the technique of trance, the first in the form of an address to two senior members of the Society of the Inner Light at the time, with Dion Fortune as the medium, (or Pythoness), wherein the Master gives an account of his own perspective on mediumship and its purpose, justification and difficulties.

Technique of Trance

October 27th 1944 7.53 - 10.05 p.m.

Very glad of opportunity of going into matter. You must understand definite limitations to this method of communication. It is the failure to appreciate this that leads to much trouble. Moreover, I am neither omniscient nor omnipotent. My jurisdiction has its limits and I am subject to those higher than myself. The Masters are looked upon as Gods but this is superstition. We are the Elder Brethren. As you are now we have been; as we are now you shall be if you can tread the path that leads thereto. (I will put aside the negative aspect of the matter for the moment and deal with its positive aspect.)

Let us consider the conditions which enable what is called mediumistic communication to take place. Take a person in whom the directive power of consciousness can be cut out and you have the condition for mediumship. There are three ways in which this can happen:

(1) Through a splitting of the mind into its component parts.
(2) Through a concentration so intense that the mind is stilled.
(3) Through a concentration so intense on the personality of the communicator that consciousness is identified therewith.

In the first state the mirror-like mind reflects all that passes before it on the astral plane. (This is another name for the Earth Soul.)

In the second state the subconscious mind is in communication with the superconscious mind.

The third state is the method we use in communication. The medium concentrates on the mental image of the communicator but persons can concentrate on mental images without necessarily becoming the vehicles of mediumistic communication. For communication to take place the communicator has to build the mental image on which the medium concentrates.

In the second type of trance communication is only received from the higher self of the medium.

In the first type any and every image is reflected without any selective power. The thoughts of the living, the thought-forms in the mental atmosphere, the images in the consciousness of any kind of being on the inner planes, all these can be reflected by the mirror-like consciousness of the passive trance.

The third type of trance is that used in the Mysteries for giving teaching and instruction, but impressions can be picked up in a random manner among a multiplicity of other impressions by the first type of mediumship. The mirror medium *can* give impressions of communications from higher sources but it is rare and is not used except in an emergency.

In the second type of trance if the Higher Self is of the grade of a Master the personality receives communications in this state from the higher planes.

It is the third state we are using and we will, therefore, put aside the consideration of the two other states to consider this in detail.

The condition of the medium is that of a hypnotised subject with the hypnotist on the inner planes communicating telepathically. What is known as hypnotism thus applies to this state. The appeal is made to the imagination and the subject is caused to imagine that he is the communicator. But lunatics do this and then some simple person thinks he constitutes himself Napoleon by standing with his hand thrust into his buttoned-up jacket. But this does not enable him to direct an army in battle. He has merely reproduced as much of the Napoleon image as he can understand. He has the ambition and love of power of Napoleon or he would not choose this image but he has not got the genius of Napoleon. There is not in him in fact the raw material for the making of a Napoleon.

Those whom the Masters select for training in Cosmic mediumship must have in them the raw material for the making of a Master.

Only enough Cosmic mediums are developed to enable communication to be maintained because it is a condition which involves great sacrifices on the part of the medium and delays their development. If this woman we are considering, *(i.e. the medium: D.F.)*, had elected not to serve thus but to develop her own personal work she could have been one of the outstanding figures of her generation. But she accepted this particular service and in consequence her history has been otherwise. She is a Pythoness of the Temple of the Mysteries and has suffered much from unskilful handling and unsatisfactory conditions. It could not be avoided. It is a problem which always has to be faced in developing Cosmic mediums. The early stages are exceedingly difficult and dangerous. The conditions of communication have to be built up and this has to be done while communication is as yet very uncertain. The cutting out of the directive power of consciousness in order to use the contents of the subconscious mind tends to induce a looseness of cohesion between the levels of the mind. Mediumship is not good for the person who practises it.

For teaching to be given in a clear and concrete form the consciousness of the medium must be highly developed so that a suitable vehicle exists for use by the communicating entity. There must be a wide range of ideas, knowledge and words available for use by the communicator. This very seldom goes with the power to become passive and permit the mental contents to be used by another intelligence.

Secondly, the emotions need to be calm and still when mediumship is being practised. So that in addition to a highly developed mind there must be a purified and harmonised nature.

These then are the conditions of satisfactory Cosmic mediumship and they are not easily attained. We have to do the best we can while the medium is being developed, unless that medium is being properly trained in a temple of the Mysteries. In the present instance communication between the Masters on the inner planes and the Mystery Tradition had broken down in the West and with infinite difficulty and many failures was and still is being re-established. Hence the Cosmic mediums had to be developed outside the necessary Temple conditions and many unfortunate incidents occurred the consequences of which you no doubt have heard. The imperfections of character of the channels of communication are only too well known. These imperfections occurred owing to the development of mediumship under adverse conditions.

It is possible to develop a person as a medium and nothing else and that is the traditional method with the Pythonesses but owing to the paucity of material in modern times persons have to be both medium and magician and this combination presents very difficult problems. They have to be magicians in order to make the conditions in which they can work as mediums.

The Pythoness for her working needs a High Priest to direct her and a circle of the priesthood to support her. These are trained initiates and somebody has to train them. In a well established Tradition each generation of the Priesthood trains the next and Pythonesses are picked from among them. But when the Tradition has broken down conditions have to be re-established through a mediumistic person who has neither director nor supporting circle.

The Masters communicating have to use the Medium to train a supporting circle and then select and train a directing High Priest from the circle, and while this process is going on the Pythoness has inadequate protection and direction.

If the mediumistic person survives long enough a proper Temple is established and the position becomes stabilised and continuous. But the history of the modern Mysteries is strewn with the wreckage of Temples in process of building around mediums who have not survived but fallen by the way.

In the light of what I have told you can doubtless understand much in the history of the Fraternity of the Inner Light which must have been perplexing to you. The late MacGregor Mathers developed his temple without any assistance on the physical plane save from his study of tradition. He did a great work but it had many flaws.

The present Pythoness we are using had some training in this very imperfect Tradition which was rapidly disintegrating owing to its flaws and as it broke up she brought the living Tradition into the new Temple like the Atlanteans' emigration into Egypt. Since then it has been one long struggle to keep open communications and to make the conditions in which she could be developed. There have been times when only a very slender link existed.

Some of the matters raised in this address were pursued in conversation at a slightly later date, on 5th December 1944, which I have lightly edited to remove the minor repetitions of impromptu verbal interchange together with some personal irrelevancies.

Q: I would like to ask how is the clarity and ease of communication affected by tides - either of the moon or of the sun?

A: Affected very little in the case of a well developed Pythoness under Temple conditions.

Q: Very little effect if we had the insulated conditions?

A: If you had a good group working with your Pythoness and seals properly put on, you are affected very little in dealing with the spiritual and mental planes - you are only affected as the Pythoness is affected. But it is a different matter if you are getting Elemental contacts - then you are affected.

Q: Could you enlarge on that?

A: Well they would only come on suitable tides. For instance, you could not set out to try for Elemental contacts on an unsuitable tide, and broadly speaking the first move in Elemental contacts comes from the inner planes so that the choice of tides is not yours - it takes care of itself. But for spiritual and intellectual teaching the Elemental tides have no appreciable effect beyond the manner in which the Pythoness reacts to them.

Q: Is there any way in which we can help the conditions for trance by the preparation of the atmosphere in the place where the trance is held?

A: Yes. First of all the physical conditions. The even temperature, dim light, freedom from interruption. These are the essential basis and not only must your medium be relaxed and comfortable, so that there is no distraction from physical discomfort, but the members of the circle should be equally at ease.

With regard to the preparation of the room I think I will deal with the formation of the circle, because the preparation of the room arises out of that. Now for the formation of your circle the individuals forming it must be, as you know, carefully chosen when it is a small circle.

Now there is a peculiarity. It is possible to bring one person into say a meeting of two or three, who is alien to the trance method, because if there is only one person to deal with, the communicator is able to cope with him, but if you bring one stronger or unsuitable person into a circle it is much more difficult to cope with.

I will explain. Supposing we have only one person present, (apart from the scribe) with whom I am communicating. The communicator can deal quite effectively with that one listener without any difficulty. If that person is limited, difficult, or in any way inexperienced - the communicator can cope with the situation.

Now the next condition would be where you have one visitor, we will call the newcomer, and a scribe, and someone in charge of the medium. Now we don't count the scribe any more than we count the medium, so you would call that a two person séance. Now there a stranger is quite manageable by the communicator. Under such circumstances he would not want to have a strange sitter and a strange scribe; and you would not want to have the scribe in charge of the sitter or the trance because the scribe has to be concentrating on the work of taking down and not in supervising the sitter. You would, therefore, have an experienced person in charge of the meeting.

Now if you go beyond the number three it becomes a circle. So that you see there is polarity working at which only one person is present; there is triangle working in which there are two sitters and scribe (or one of the two, if both experienced, can act as scribe.)

Now in circle working everybody must be carefully chosen and experienced sitters, with the exception of the newcomer being introduced. You can introduce strangers one at a time. No more, because the communicator has got to make contact with the sitter. It is very necessary that the sitters should be of one mind in one place, so they must be carefully chosen, and each newcomer must be carefully built into the circle.

Now I will give you one or two examples from past experience of difficulties that have arisen from disregarding these rules. Sometimes it was impossible to avoid disregarding them but we can be on our guard in future.

Now with regard to being of one mind in one place do you remember a certain circle working in which two members were present who resigned the next day, and who clearly had it in their minds to withdraw then. Now the presence of those two persons prevented deep trance from being established because your circle had a break in it. Therefore the trance was purely superficial, there was no real contact between the communicator and the circle.

I was the communicator on that occasion, and the impression I got was of speaking to a vacuum. It was a very curious impression. I had the medium well in hand and I knew the scribe was taking down. I could not be sure if there was anybody else in the room or not, or alternatively, whether it could be people overhearing.

I thought people were overhearing, and you will recall that I gave a very non-committal address on that occasion. I knew that those who were overhearing were initiates, but I knew that whoever they were they should not have been there. I did not care to investigate in the circumstances because I did not know who was present, or who was not present, so having started I went through with it and gave a non-committal address.

In the case of visitors we occasionally invite for special purposes, then it is best to have one person and the scribe only present; not to bring them into a circle. It is much easier for the communicator to deal with them under such circumstances.

Q: Why is that?

A: Because if you have a circle, when that circle is properly formed it forms a single unit, and the communicator deals with it as a unit, and cannot give the necessary attention to the visitor. The visitor has to take his chance, more or less, in the circle; so when a newcomer is being introduced it is best to have the person in charge of the Pythoness and the scribe only present while the communicator gets to know them - the same as a visitor. Then when the communicator has established contact, a person who is to become a working unit in the circle, can, at another sitting, be introduced to their place in the circle.

Q: You spoke of triangle working and of circle working. Apart from the necessity of being of one mind in one place, which is the spiritual attitude, is there any aura technique, in the sense of opening certain centres, that the sitters might be well advised or instructed upon?

A: No, not at the present stage of our work, and in any case it is not used in circle working, it is used in magic in the Greater Mysteries. And in any case, it is only used by persons who have had a thorough training in polarity working. The opening of the centres is not done in circle working. What you get in the group circle working is the pooling of auras, which is quite a different matter. That means the unreserved dedication and it means that the persons concerned open their auras, so that you get one aura only, not a number of individual auras. In circle working you have a single aura which is like a vast personality, and to achieve that the persons concerned open their auras.

Q: Does the same thing apply to triangle working?

A: Yes, but it is much easier in triangle working. In polarity working the two persons make one aura, whether the second person is on the physical or the inner planes makes no difference. In triangle working the same thing happens, and if the apex of the triangle, in the triangle working, is a Master on the inner planes, it means a very great deal to the persons concerned to share auras with him, and the same thing applies to circle working. For the communication of teaching which is being written down for the instruction of the brethren, the triangle is the most useful form of working because the teaching given is limited by the capacity of the least developed person present.

Q: That applies to both triangle and circle working?

A: Yes, but in the triangle you can select your persons more easily. The circle working is used not for the purpose of bringing through teaching for the brethren, but for the purpose of instructing and developing the circle.

Q: In both cases does not the actual physical attitude of the body have an effect of the opening of the aura, which the pooling of the auras involves? I am thinking of the physical act of crossing the legs and hands, etc.

A: Yes, you should use the same postures as you use in meditation. You want the body free from strain. Hands on thighs so that both sides of the body are balanced. This gives a balanced flow of force.

Q: You know what you send through. Do you know exactly what arrives? Can you hear yourself?

A: I know what I want to say to you. I do not, of course, know what is written down by the scribe. But what you are asking,

I take it, is this. Supposing conditions of communication are not good, then do I know how much comes through or how much does not?

Now if I tell you how a trance appears from my side perhaps you will understand better. If communication is good I get right through and have the impression that I am in the room talking to you. I am quite unaware of the medium.

Supposing the trance is not going well, then I have a peculiar sensation - how can I describe it to you? It is like working with a tool which is loose in its socket. You know what it is like when you work with a tool loose in its socket?

Q: Yes, but as far as I can remember, you have not told us to improve the conditions while a trance is in progress.

A: That is another point. If the conditions are not good I am not clearly aware of what the conditions are like. It is like being in a fog, you see. One does not know necessarily what is wrong, one only knows the communications are not good. You are trying to find out what is the margin of error in trance communications are you not?

Very well now, the conditions prevailing on your side, that is to say if the medium is not in deep trance or the reception is not good, that inhibits, but you will not get actually misleading or distorted teaching. Do you understand my meaning?

Q: Yes. Is the depth of trance in your control?

A: No, that is the difficulty, and when trance is poor I cannot explain to you, and cannot see what is happening. I am in a fog and I am working with a tool loose in its socket.

Q: But when one works with a tool loose in its socket one knows the results.

A: Yes, but unfortunately not until after it has happened. It is improbable I could improve a bad trance at the time - unless the trance deepens which it sometimes does. And you see, once trance communication has been established one is very reluctant to break it off abruptly for there is an element of shock for both the medium and the sitter. It is better to let the trance run its course naturally rather than break it off unless there is a very good reason for doing so.

Q: Does communication depend then: (1) on the spiritual development of the Pythoness, (2) upon her magical organisation - her actual psychic condition, as to the depth of trance or possibilities of communication from a higher or lower plane, and also the logical and smooth communication of what is being said?

A: Well now, all these factors come in different proportions. First of all mediumship is a purely psychic factor, neither spiritual nor mental in itself, but high spiritual teachings can only be brought through in their pure form, that is to say not translated into symbolism, by a person of high spiritual development.

High intellectual instruction can only be brought through a person who has got the words and ideas available in their consciousness. Communications are restricted by the capacity of the medium, but mediumship is a psychic factor depending neither upon spiritual nor intellectual factors.

Q: It is the function of the priest, then, is it not, to protect and enable the development of the Pythoness?

A: Yes, to develop, protect and direct.

Q: Do I understand you to say that mediumship is purely a question of getting into a certain condition, yet at the same time the equipment of the medium can inhibit or not allow to come through, say, a certain kind of teaching?

A: The equipment of the medium determines the degree of the teaching that comes through, the equipment of the communicator determines the kind of teaching that comes through.

Q: What do you mean by degree?

A: Whether the teaching is simple or advanced.

Q: When you say the kind of teaching, are you referring to the plane of the teaching?

A: No, the Ray. Elemental, devotional, Hermetic, whatever it may be.

Q: But cannot an attitude in the medium inhibit even the kind of teaching that comes through?

A: Yes, the medium has to be in sympathy. An atheistical medium could not transmit devotional teaching.

Q: Would it be right to put it this way? That with regard to the kind of teaching that comes through the medium should be both consciously and subconsciously "tabula rasa", but with regard to the degree of the teaching, its logical development, its contact with current thought and so on, that depends upon the equipment of the medium.

A: You want a medium with a well informed mind, a good vocabulary too, free from strong prejudice or emotional bias that will distort.

Q: Does the emotional attitude of the medium inhibit or close the doors in any way?

A: If the medium is afraid of a certain line of investigation or disapproves thereof, it will close that particular door. What is wanted is a medium with a well furnished and open mind. Any strong pre-determinations on the part of the medium inhibit.

Q: And a balanced nature?

A: That of course is essential to emotional serenity. Any bias that the medium may have will exercise a selective influence over the communications coming through. The medium will be open for the transmission of one type of teaching, closed against another - and that can be very misleading and can result in a very one-sided body of teaching.

Q: You use the ideas and images which are stocked in the medium's mind. Would it be any extra difficulty for you to give, say, historical teaching of which the medium has not heard?

A: No, because one pieces it together out of the known material. After all, words are common property, are they not?

Q: So you work with words as well as ideas?

A: Yes and no. For instance, if spiritual or philosophical teaching is being given, and the proper words are not available, images and circumlocutions have to be used.

Q: Yes, it is quite noticeable at times that there is the transmission of words and ideas and you use the words and ideas of the medium. There is also the transmission of power.

A: Well now, that is another point you are raising. We are clearing ground at the moment by asking and answering questions. This enables me to see what the problems are. Take my own case, for instance, who am used to using this medium - I communicate with words and ideas. Another communicator, who is not so used to the medium, or who has not got an English vocabulary, will use ideas which are translated in the medium's mind and presented thereby.

Q: Was that the case of the communication of "The Cosmic Doctrine" made by him whom we knew as "the Old Greek"?

A: I acted as communicator from a very much greater mind than mine. That happens on occasion. You must remember that in those days we had a very much less developed medium to deal with. When you get a strong sense of the personality of the communicator you know that communication is well established and that the personality is actually inside the mind of the medium, but where communication is not so well developed the ideas are, as it were, thrown upon the mirror of the medium's mind and reflected therefrom.

Q: Well now, you have referred to the degree and kind of teaching - the kind being determined by yourself or the communicator; but you have also referred to the need for some opening to be made from this side - using the analogy of the cable or the life rope - as if you could not get through without some opening.

A: Well now, there are three factors concerned.

i) The communicator.
ii) The medium.
iii) The persons concerned.

The medium is operated by the persons receiving the communication. The communicator has to await the opportunity afforded.

Q: You mean to say that if a trance starts and you wish to send through a certain message you would be unable to do so unless you were given an opening from this side?

A: Working with those now present you have a mental attitude which would give me an opening, but supposing the medium went into trance for some complete strangers, I should not get the chance to give the message I wanted.

Q: Is not that mental attitude similar to the opening of the auric centres?

A: No, that is a magical business you are talking about; what we are dealing with now is a mental business - on a different plane.

Q: In that connection you said to me the other day in the course of a conversation that the conditions were harmonious but that there was not much power. How does the magical condition of the sitters affect what comes through the trance?

A: Well the amount of power available depends mainly on the medium, on her mental or physical condition, but it can be inhibited or, rather, neutralised, by bad conditions in the circle. The medium might be in a very good condition physically, mentally or emotionally, but if you have light minded sitters it will affect the communication.

I may be able to give you some more consecutive teaching. I don't know how much you know or how much you don't know, but remember there are three factors - the communicator, the medium, the circle or the sitters, and each one contributes a modicum.

However good conditions may be, if the medium is not well, or disturbed, or tired, the communicator will lack the necessary power to communicate.

However good the medium might be, if the circle is not all it might be, the contact does not come through well.

Or you may get a communicator of exceptional power who will put through more force than the average if conditions are suitable. Communicators vary in power.

Q: Is it reasonable to assume that on the inner planes each communicator is pretty well constant?

A: Yes, except that the communicators evolve as well as the sitters. My position now is very different from what it was when I served the person who was referred to as "the Old Greek".

Q: In so short a time?

A: What is time? Time is measured by us by what happens, not by the number of times the earth turns on its axis.

Q: Time is a question of experience, is it not?

A: Depends on your level. On one level yes, on another level it links up with the evolution of the solar system. It depends on your level.

And this final reply: "It depends on your level" would seem to be an apt response to many questions with regard to spiritualism and occultism and to the various grades of communication to be found within each of them.

PART THREE

THE INHABITANTS OF THE UNSEEN

Whoever contacts the invisible world, whether by means of his own psychism or by employing the psychism of another as a channel of evocation, has need of some system of classification in order that he may be able to understand the varied phenomena with which he will meet. Not all of them are due to the spirits of the departed; there are other denizens of the invisible world than those who have once had human form. Nor are all the phenomena due to the subconscious mind entirely subjective. Confusion arises when that which should be assigned to one division is allocated to another. It can be clearly shown that the explanation which is offered does not account for the facts. Nevertheless, the facts are not disposed of by showing the explanation to be fallacious. A correct classification would yield an explanation which can stand up to any impartial investigation and be justified of its wisdom.

The classification which it is proposed to employ in these pages is drawn largely from the traditional occult sources, and it is believed that it will throw light on certain experiences met with by psychic research workers. It is offered in a spirit of cooperation, as independent testimony to a common experience.

The Souls of the Departed

Of all the inhabitants of the invisible worlds, the ones with which it is easiest for us to get into touch are the souls of human beings who have shed their outer garment of flesh, either temporarily or permanently. Any one who is familiar with spiritualistic or esoteric thought soon becomes habituated to the idea that a man is not changed by death. The personality remains; it is only the body that is gone.

The esotericist, in his concept of the nature of departed souls, distinguishes between those who are going through the inter-natal phase, that is to say, who are living in the non-physical worlds between incarnations, and those who will not reincarnate again. There is a great difference in capacity and outlook between these two types of souls, and many of the issues at present outstanding between spiritualism and occultism are undoubtedly due to a failure to recognise this fact.

The occultist does not maintain that existence is an eternal sequence of birth and death, but that at a certain phase of evolution the soul enters upon a series of material lives, and through the development made during these lives, it finally outgrows the mundane phase of evolution, becoming more and more spiritualised towards the end of this period, until finally it wins its freedom from matter and reincarnates no more, continuing its existence as a disembodied spirit with a human mind. Mentality, the occultist maintains, can only be obtained through incarnation in human form. Those beings who have not undergone this experience have not got mentality as we understand it, with certain exceptions which we will consider later.

For the most part, it is the souls of the living dead who are contacted in the séance room. Liberated souls go on to their own place and are not so easily reached. Only those return within range of the earth sphere who have some business there. The discussion of this point would open up a vast field of interest which we cannot deal with at the moment. It must suffice to say that, as is well known to all workers in psychic research, there are souls of a higher type than those commonly encountered, who are concerned with the evolution of humanity and the training of those who are willing to cooperate with them in their work.

We may say, then, that the souls of the departed may be divided into three types:

i) the souls of the living dead, who will return again to the earth life.

ii) liberated souls, who have outgrown earth life and have gone on to another sphere of existence.

iii) liberated souls, who, having gone on, return again to the earth sphere because they have work to do therein.

A recognition of these three types of departed souls will serve to explain many of the discrepancies we encounter between the statements of spiritualists and occultists. The occultist aims chiefly at getting into touch with the returning souls for the purposes of specific work in which both he and they are concerned; for the most part, he leaves the souls of the living dead severely alone. Personally, I am of the opinion that he is mistaken in so doing. It is quite true that they can be of little assistance to him in his chosen work, but the normal companionship of the living with the dead robs death of most of its terrors and is steadily building a bridge between those who remain and those who have passed over. The occultist should certainly not invite the cooperation of the living dead as he would that of the returning souls, for they have their own work to do; nor can he place as much reliance on their knowledge and insight as on that of those who are freed from the wheel of birth and death; neither has he any right to try to use them as he would elemental spirits in the course of his experiments. Admitting these qualifications, however, there seems no reason why the occultist should not share in the interchange of amenities which is continually taking place across the borderline. After all, death is one of the processes of life, and the dead are very much alive and quite normal.

Projections of the Living

The appearance of a simulacrum of a human being at the point of death is exceedingly common, and innumerable well attested instances exist of its occurrence. It is not so well known, however, that it is possible for the simulacrum, or astro-etheric form, to be projected voluntarily by the trained occultist. Such projections, in proportion to the hosts of disembodied souls encountered when the threshold is crossed, are exceedingly rare; nevertheless they occur, and may be met with, therefore they must be included in any classification which aims at being comprehensive. Usually such a projected soul appears to be entirely occupied with its own affairs and in a state of absorption which causes it to appear to ignore its surroundings. As a matter of fact, it most frequently happens that the disembodied spirit has its work cut out to maintain consciousness at all on the higher planes, and its self-absorption is that of the beginner on a bicycle. Occasionally communication may be established between such a projected etheric body and a group of experimenters, and very interesting results are obtained; but unless there is sufficient materialisation to render the simulacrum visible to the non-psychic, the experiment will partake rather of the nature of telepathy grafted upon mediumship than of a true projection of the astro-etheric form. Such visitants are neither angels nor devils but "human, all too human."

The Angelic Hierarchies

The average Protestant has a very dim notion concerning the angelic hierarchies, the great hosts of beings of another evolution than ours, though children of the same Heavenly Father. The Qabalah, however, is explicit on this point, and classifies them into ten archangels and ten orders of angelic beings. Buddhist, Hindu, and Mohammedan theologies are equally explicit. We may therefore reckon that in this agreement of witnesses there is surety of testimony, and it may serve our purpose best to take for our guide that system from which Christianity took its rise - mystic Judaism.

We will not go into the elaborate classifications employed by the Jewish rabbis, which have their importance for purposes of magic but are not germane to our present issue. It is quite enough that we realise that there are divinely created beings of varying degrees of greatness, from the mighty archangel whom St John the Divine saw standing in the sun, down to the nameless heavenly messengers who have from time to time visited mankind.

Second the spheres to which are assigned the disembodied spirits of humanity dwell these heavenly beings, and in some high range of spiritual light the psychic or medium sometimes touches them. In the Vale Owen scripts there is much concerning them that is of great interest.

It is said by the rabbis that these beings are perfect, each after his kind; but they do not evolve, and it is noticeable that they are non-intellectual. One might almost call them divine robots, each strictly conditioned by its own nature perfectly to fulfil the office for which it was created; free from all struggle and inner conflict, but changeless, and therefore unevolving.

No angel, it is said, ever goes outside his own sphere of activity. The angel who "has healing in his wings" cannot bestow visions, nor the bestower of visions serve as the strong guard against the powers of darkness.

Esotericists make a fundamental distinction between angels and the souls of men. They say that the divine sparks, which are the nuclei of the souls of men, proceed from the noumenal cosmos, from the same plane whereon the Solar Logos has His being. They are therefore of the same innermost nature as the Godhead. Angels, on the other hand, are created by the Solar Logos as the first of His created beings. They neither fall into generation, nor rise by regeneration, but remain in changeless but unevolving perfection till the end of the epoch.

The functions of the angels are diverse, and cannot be entered upon here in detail. They are, each according to his office and rank, God's messengers in things of the spirit, but they have no direct contact with dense matter. That office is performed by another order of beings altogether, the elementals, who differ in origin and inmost nature from both angels and men.

Elementals

Much confusion of thought exists concerning the order of beings known as elementals. They are sometimes confused with the spirits of men. Undoubtedly many happenings attributed to spirits are to be assigned to the activities of these other orders of beings. Again, they are not to be confused with the evil demons, or, to give them the Qabalistic name, the Qlipphoth.

Elementals are the thought-forms generated by co-ordinated systems of reactions that have become stereotypes by constant and unchanging repetition. Some explanation is necessary to make this concept clear, and we shall understand it best if we survey the means by which elementals come into being.

Each epoch of evolution is constituted by the outgoing and return of a life-wave of living souls. These are referred to in esoteric terminology as the Lords of Flame, of Form, and of Mind. The present evolution will become the Lords of Humanity. Each life-wave develops its characteristic contribution to evolution. When the Divine sparks which constituted the nuclei of the evolving souls of each evolution are withdrawn back up the planes and reabsorbed into the Kingdom of God, their work remains behind them in that which they have builded, whether it be the chemical elements evolved by the Lords of Form, the chemical reactions evolved by the Lords of Flame, or the reactions of consciousness evolved by the Lords of Mind.

Humanity, it is held, is evolving the power of co-ordinated consciousness, and the Lords of Humanity therefore hold the same relationship to the Lords of Mind that the Lords of Flame hold to the Lords of Form. These beings, however, of the three earlier life-waves, have passed out of range of the life of our earth, each group to its appropriate planet, and the Lords of Humanity are still absorbed in the task of building and have not yet, save those few who have become Masters, escaped from the bondage of the material in which they work. Consequently, it is but rarely that any psychic save the higher grades of adept ever contacts any of these beings.

They have left behind them, however, as has already been noted, the forms which they built up in the course of their evolution. These forms, as psychics teach, actually consist of co-ordinated systems of magnetic stresses. Whenever any movement takes place an electric current is set up, and if the series of co-ordinated movements is repeated many times, these currents tend to make adjustments among themselves and become co-ordinated on their own account, quite independently of the physical forms whose activities gave rise to them. It is out of these coordinations that the elementals are evolved.

We cannot go more deeply into this most interesting and intricate subject in the present pages. It is a matter for a separate study. Enough has been said, however, to indicate that although the ultimate product of the evolution of the angelic, the human, and the elemental kingdom is to produce consciousness and intelligence, the origin of the three types of beings is entirely different, and so also is their destiny.

The divine sparks are the emanations of the Great Unmanifest, Ain Soph Aur, in the terminology of the Qabalists; the angels are the creations of the Solar Logos, and the elementals are "the creations of the created," that is to say, they are developed out of the activities of the material universe.

Of the elementals thus evolved there are many types. Firstly, the four great divisions of the elemental spirits of Earth, Air, Fire, and Water, known respectively to the Alchemists as Gnomes, Sylphs, Salamanders, and Undines. These really represent four types of activity arising out of four types of relationship. In solids (the element of Earth) the molecules adhere together. In liquids (the element of Water) the molecules are free moving. In gases (the element of Air) they repel each other and therefore diffuse to their uttermost limits. And in Fire, the essential property of its activity is to change plane, or transmute. The four kingdoms of primary elementals under their angelic kings represent the co-ordinated, purposive, and intelligent action of these four properties of matter - the mind side of the material phenomena, to be precise.

This fact is well known to occultists, and they employ the mind side of matter in their magical work. Consequently many of these elemental systems of reactions have, as it were, been domesticated by adepts. Elementals thus domesticated become imbued with consciousness of a human type. These developed (or initiated) elementals are sometimes met with by psychics.

We are now trenching upon some of the most secret aspects of occultism, and not a great deal can be said; and even if it were said, little of it would be understood save by those who were already well versed in esoteric science.

Nature Spirits

Wherever any set of natural objects is essentially a unit, an oversoul develops by the same method we have already considered with regard to the evolution of elementals. But as the term elemental is usually reserved for the spirits of the four elements, it is as well to employ a different term to describe these oversouls, for they are essentially different. The elementals evolve from elemental substance, that is to say, from the etheric existence which was the fore-runner of dense matter. Nature spirits, however, evolve from the co-ordination of many complex forms which have a certain factor in common. For instance, an oversoul is developed by a forest, or a mountain. These oversouls are psychic units, built up out of the innumerable co-ordinated reactions made by the forest as a whole, to their respective not-selves. Any cleft in the mountain, any glade in the forest, so long as it is sufficiently differentiated to function as a unit and have definite lines of demarcation to the not-self, develops an oversoul also. Out of this fact comes the concept of the gods of places. All sensitives readily sense the presence and nature of such oversouls.

Each species of living creatures has a similar oversoul, according to the esotericist, and many important considerations which we cannot enter upon now arise from this point. It is possible to contact the composite lion, or the composite eagle, and these entities are closely related to great psychic forces, hence the use of their symbolism in the representation of both the gods of the Egyptians and the Evangelists of the Christians.

The Qlipphoth or Demons

These beings are developed in the same way as the elementals, save that they originate in the unbalanced force which is generated as each new phase of evolution comes into existence. For there is always a transition period to be gone through as a new phase is evolved. Equilibrium cannot be established immediately and the unbalanced force tends to run riot. As far as possible it is compensated by the conscious action of the angelic hosts. This is a part of their function, but a complete compensation is practically impossible. Especially was this the case during the earlier phases of evolution, when the angelic hosts themselves were not all yet in being.

These unbalanced forces, then, form the substance of the kingdom of positive evil, as distinguished from negative evil, which is mere resistance, inertia, and has its uses. Into this kingdom of the Qlipphoth go all unbalanced forces generated by man, reinforcing the original evil.

Many of these Qlipphothic elementals have been brought under control by black magicians. It is these that form the chief danger of mediumship, and are one of the reasons why the occultist is so chary of its use, and will only employ it under definite precautions. The uninitiated psychic comparatively rarely meets a demonic intelligence, but the initiate, who has to shoulder the karma of his fraternity when he takes initiation, is liable to do so, for there are black sheep in every society, and their legacy of black magic has to be contended with by those who come after them. All the older fraternities have this problem to face in varying degrees, and therefore their neophytes are instructed to have nothing whatever to do with the séance room in case a dark familiar of one of the past brethren should take advantage of the opportunity. This is the real reason why the occultists will not work with the spiritualist. It is one of the drawbacks of admission to a fraternity, and the reason why many sensitives fear to take initiation.

The trained occultist, however, knows how to protect himself from unwanted intruders, and once he has reached psychic adulthood, does not fear them because he knows how to deal with them. The neophyte is instructed to keep out of harm's way until he is in a position to take care of himself. So long as this common sense precaution is observed, all is well, but if ambition, or curiosity, or mere ignorance cause a beginner to take risks, he may expose himself to considerable unpleasantness, to say the least of it.

It is for this reason that an occultist always draws the magic circle and works inside it. The procession of priests and acolytes round a church that is being consecrated and the Masonic custom of "squaring the Lodge" have their roots in this "magic circle" which guards against the power of darkness.

Whenever any manifestation from the Unseen is expected there should always be the "circle," the delimited sphere within which evocation takes place; never the "unconsecrated place" which permits the inrush of forces from all sides.

Thought-forms

It is difficult to know whether thought-forms should be designated beings or objects. After all, everything which has existence is a being, and though a thought-form is one of the "creations of the created," and therefore has not got noumenal existence, nevertheless, being an actuality on its own plane, it has a phenomenal existence. We may therefore not unjustifiably class them among the beings of the Unseen, especially as there are certain types of thought-forms which are very highly organised and endowed with considerable intelligence. A thought-form is an externalisation of the mind-essence of an intelligent being. Every thought that is formulated is, of course, an organisation or modelling of thought-substance, but for the most part such lightly constructed forms never get beyond the aura of the person who evolved them. An influence is radiated from them, but the actual thought-form is not extruded from the aura to take up an independent existence outside. We may make the distinction clearer by thinking of the light of a lamp shining out of a house, and the lamp itself being hurled through the window at the head of an intruder.

Only by a powerful effort is a thought-form extruded. That effort may be made spontaneously under the influence of emotion, or deliberately by an effort of will directed by the necessary knowledge. Any person in a high state of emotional tension extrudes thought-forms, but unless there is an organised idea behind them, they rapidly disintegrate. It is only when a little bit of the real self is extruded with them that they hold together and remain potent. Such ensouled forms are often spoken of as "artificial elementals." As a matter of actual fact, only a person with some mediumistic tendency can project actual thought-forms. Other folk, whose etheric substance does not readily part company with their dense body, although they may emanate strong thought-influence, will not extrude the actual elementals. It is these ensouled thought-forms extruded by a mediumistic person under emotional stress, which form the basis of many "hauntings." It must be borne in mind that at the moment of death the etheric double is withdrawn from the physical body. If, therefore, death takes place under great emotional stress, it may well happen that the thought-forms being cast off in myriads from the profoundly disturbed mind, get ensouled by etheric substance even in people who normally would not be mediumistic.

The trained occultist frequently avails himself of this little known fact. He deliberately, according to well-known laws, "magnetises" objects by projecting a portion of his etheric double, usually the etheric hand, into them. The clothes we wear are, of course, filled with our etheric emanations, but these are usually fugitive and soon evaporate unless precautions are taken. It is for this reason that the black magician tries to get hold of some portion of the clothing of his intended victim, and people who are living in countries where juju and similar rites are practised learn that it is injudicious to give cast-off clothing to servants, and highly advisable to commit all unwanted personal possessions to the flames.

A consecrated object differs from a magnetised one in that the force employed for its ensouling is not that of the operator, but of a non-material entity which is invoked to descend upon it. A talisman may be consecrated to Mars with due ceremony, just as a crucifix may be consecrated to Christ. There is no difference in principle between the two consecrations, though different types of force are invoked and the resulting talisman or amulet is potent for different purposes. We had better realise that the ceremonial aspect of Christianity is purely magical, and that that is nothing against it. Ceremonial magic is not necessarily the evocation of devils. The Eucharist is a magical ceremonial for evoking the Christ. Ceremonial is a psychological method, nothing more or less.

Thought-forms are sometimes extruded apart from intense emotion. If a mental image be repeatedly visualised and brooded over, it tends to take up an independent existence. Such a thought-form may receive ensoulment from many different sources, attracting to itself that which is congenial to its nature. For instance, a long-brooded thought of hate might attract a Qlipphothic demon, a long-brooded thought of love might attract one of the higher elementals or even an angelic presence. These, however, would not, except in very rare cases, when the work was done deliberately by a magician, actually enter into and embody themselves in the thought-form, but rather extrude a portion of their substance into it. Such a thought-form has a very peculiar existence, being endowed with life by the non-human contact and with intelligence by its human contact. Several interesting stories have been written having this fact for a theme. The invisible playmates of children are not infrequently thought-forms thus ensouled.

This brief survey makes no attempt at any detailed description. No more than an enumeration has been aimed at. It may serve, however, to give some indication of the different types of being that may be discerned on the Inner Planes and to convey some idea of the exceeding variety of the life of those regions. The planes lie one above the other in successive spheres of consciousness and as we rise upon them, we contact first one, and then another type of being. This accounts for the divergent reports given by different seers. They are not necessarily untrue because they do not agree with each other; it may be that they are describing different spheres of the Unseen. The value of the traditional occult cosmogony is very great to all those engaged in investigating the subtler planes of existence, for it gives a bird's eye view of the whole and enables things to be correlated and seen in proportion and perspective. Without such a comprehensive survey, psychic science is in the same position as biology before the advent of Darwin. A mass of data had been observed, but no valid general laws had been deduced. So it is with psychic science; it has observed well its data, but the time has now come when that data must be classified and expressed in formulae. Psychic science will be well-advised to take counsel with the traditional wisdom of the initiates when it sets out upon this task, for there may be found the fruits of centuries of experience. If that age-old experience of occult science be mated to the scientific methods of the best school of psychic research, the progeny should be a light to the nations.

COMMENTARY

As Dion Fortune makes plain in her April 1938 article she regards her contacts to be Masters, that is to say beings somewhat out of the normal run of deceased friends or relatives. They also appear to be responsible for certain inner plane functions apart from their dedication to teaching on esoteric subjects. In one respect this marks a great divide between occultism and spiritualism although the division is by no means an absolutely cut and dried one because in spiritualist circles there are also teachers, often referred to as Guides, whose teaching is more philosophical than the passing of personal messages. Stainton Moses' "Imperator" was one of the first of these, since when others have followed, often with Red Indian names: White Eagle and Silver Birch perhaps being the most well known. There has always been some speculation and discussion as to exactly who or what the Masters are, as defined by different schools and contacts.

In the columns of "The Inner Light" magazine for March and April 1938 Dion Fortune took pains to explain further what she meant by them in terms of her experience.

Who Are The Masters?

In the early days of the Fraternity of the Inner Light, when it was of the dimensions of a family party, there was no need to put on paper any explanation of the nature of "The Masters", or the relationship of the Fraternity to them, because all who took part in the work of the Fraternity had personal knowledge of both these matters. Now, however, that our organisation has grown far beyond the "happy family party" stage, it is as well to state clearly what is implied by the brief phrase in our literature that announces the connection of the Fraternity with the Masters.

First let us consider who and what the Masters may be. They

have been called super-men, and that is a term which is both descriptive and satisfactory. It has, however, been loosely used in occult literature and made to include persons in incarnation who should more properly be termed adepts, as well as beings of other orders of evolution than the human, who should properly be distinguished as angels or elementals according to grade and type. As the word is used in these pages it indicates human souls who have passed beyond adepthood and are not in incarnation. In order to understand the nature and place in the hierarchy of things of these super-men it is necessary to consider them in relation to the scheme of initiation, of which they are the crown and completion.

Those who are familiar with the doctrine of reincarnation know that the soul evolves through a series of incarnations till it reaches the state of development when it no longer needs the discipline of the plane of form, having learnt all the lessons that physical life can teach. In due course the whole of evolution will reach this stage, just as it has reached the stage of individualisation in matter; there are, however, always those who by their intensive development draw ahead of the crowd. This intensive development is attained through self-discipline and mind-training, and it is the gradually accumulated tradition of the technique of this process which constitutes the Mysteries. Those who undertake this training are called seekers, servers, dedicands, initiates and adepts according to the degree of development they have attained.

It takes more than one life of Mystery-training to reach the higher grades beyond that of dedicand, which is the grade of those who have sought and served and whose dedication has been accepted after the tests of faithful service have been passed. Up to this grade advancement depends on character; however fine the intellect may be, it will not take people through these grades. For the grades of initiate and adept and their sub-divisions, intellect and strength are necessary, for character alone, however noble, will not take one beyond the grades that serve. In those grades, however, the foundations can be laid that in another life will take one into the grades of knowledge and power. The combination of character and knowledge gives the wisdom which is the characteristic of the initiate, but only the combination of character, knowledge and power gives adepthood.

In the grade of Seeker, the student learns the theory and philosophy of occult science; in the grade of Server he learns to live the life of the Path; these two grades are not conferred by ritual or revealed by teaching but are stages in the development of the soul. Some people are widely read in esoteric literature, but make no practical use of their knowledge beyond a desultory interest in so-called super-normal phenomena; there are other people who lead truly dedicated lives who have no knowledge of the philosophy of the higher life; neither of these can be said to be upon the Path. Only those who realise the practical applications of the Ancient Wisdom and rule their lives accordingly can be said to be treading that Path which is as narrow as the edge of a sword and as straight as its blade.

The Ancient Wisdom teaches that all things issue from a single source, are ruled by a common law, and are of such undivided substance that what affects a part inevitably affects the whole, spreading through it like ripples over water; though each unit consciousness is an individualised entity, it has been built up on the common basis of the One Life which it shares with all creation; one might liken it to a mountain peak, separate in itself, but rising from the common level of rock with the rest of the range.

If this knowledge be realised and not merely apprehended, it must of necessity modify our attitude towards our fellow beings; and with the realisation comes a sensation - the sensation of the one-ness of all life. Consciousness extends to the level where all are one, and we realise the terrible truth of the words that all creation groaneth and travaileth together. It is an actual fact of experience that those who have touched this level of consciousness react to the stresses of national life. Equally, however, from the same level they draw upon the sources of national energy and by the very fact of their existence and the experiences they pass through, play a not unimportant part in influencing the life of the race to which they belong. It is for this reason that genuine initiates of the Mysteries never take part in politics - they have no need to - their inner spiritual experiences become part of the racial group mind and exert a profound influence upon the subconscious elements of racial life that form the unrealised background of each individual consciousness.

When this re-orientation towards life has taken place, so that a man or woman lives as part of a larger whole and not as an uncorrelated unit, with all of competition and confusion that that implies, the next stage opens up - the stage of the dedicand, the person whose dedication is accepted. This marks a turning-point in the evolution of the soul, for now is the time when the traditional technique of spiritual culture can properly be taught; to teach it before this stage is reached is like weaning a child too soon. If knowledge is obtained when the spirit of dedication is lacking, the temptation to abuse it is very great; and even if the spirit of dedication is there, the soul needs the discipline of service before it can trust its own self-control.

The dedicand learns after the manner of an apprentice by working alongside a skilled craftsman. There is no other way in which the unfoldment of the higher levels of consciousness can be brought about. Sympathetic induction of vibration enables the gulf to be crossed that is well-nigh impassable to the unaided. People often dispute this, and declare that it should not be so, but it is a matter of experience that contact with a person who has the higher consciousness awakens the higher consciousness with a rapidity and certainty that is lacking in even the best of correspondence courses. It is possible, however, to obtain this awakening of the higher vibrations by reading a book written by one who possessed the higher consciousness, it can also be obtained by visiting a place of power, where the higher vibrations have been evoked by those who have knowledge; but these impersonal awakenings are only possible when the soul has been upon the Path in a previous life.

Having proved his dedication by the spirit of service in which he lives his life, the person who aspires to be a dedicand has to prove his knowledge of the Ancient Wisdom by finding an initiator; if he has genuine insight into the nature of the Mystery Traditions, he will know how to look for that initiator and how to recognise him when he appears; he will follow every possible trail and clue until he finds what he seeks, and it is surprising how quickly he will achieve his goal when the right conditions prevail in his own consciousness. Having achieved, and having been accepted as a pupil by one who possesses the higher consciousness and can therefore act as an initiator, it is the duty, nay, the privilege of the dedicand to earn his training by service after the manner of an apprentice. It is not enough to contribute to funds, actual personal service must be given, because this, and this alone, brings the pupil inside the aura of the Fraternity into which the initiator will ultimately admit him.

We must now consider the question of the nature of a Fraternity. It is simply an association of people on the physical plane who are being trained themselves, and are training others, in a particular symbol-system such as is used as a method of notation in the Mystery Tradition. After a student has reached a certain degree of development he can operate any symbol-system with equal ease, and beyond that comes a stage when he can dispense with symbols altogether; but in the early stages of his training, while his mind is being accustomed to operate beyond the planes of form to which it is adapted, a symbol-system is essential to systematic and balanced development; those who have not been trained in a symbol-system lack the key to the Mystery Tradition; the richness of the treasure-house that is opened by that key can be gauged by reading such books as "The Secret Doctrine" and "The Golden Bough". Whosoever possesses the key to one symbol-system can interpret the meaning of any other, and to lack this access to tradition is a very great loss. The key simply consists in knowing how to use a symbol-system, and is taught like violin-playing, not revealed like a pass-word. It cannot, therefore, be betrayed, for a man can either use the Mystery technique, or he cannot. I have betrayed - if it is a betrayal - everything there is to betray in my book, "The Mystical Qabalah", but no one save a person with the roots of initiation in him will be any the wiser. I have not concealed any clues; in fact I have done my utmost to be explicit, but the fact remains that only the seeing eye perceives what is there to be seen.

An initiate may be taken to be a dedicated person who has been trained in a symbol-system and therefore possesses the key to the traditional wisdom of the Illuminati. There are many grades in this training, in fact the work is taught degree by degree in order that the foundations may be properly laid. But although the outer grades are given formally, with definite instruction and with ceremonial, it is the inner awakening and development that alone can lead on to adepthood; this should take place *pari passu* with the outer grades; it if does not, these grades prove abortive. One must therefore cease from further study and apply what one knows and so gain a deepening of experience. This is best obtained by fulfilling the function of teacher and helping with the training of the junior members. This function of teacher is an exceedingly important one in the Mysteries, and at each of the higher stages on the Path the initiate has to turn back and teach his juniors what he knows, thereby perfecting his own knowledge by practical experience. In fact it is a tradition of the Mysteries that no one may take a grade till he has trained his successor, and I can vouch for the truth of this from my own experiences. These laws of the Mysteries are not arbitrary rules or enactments, but like the laws of science, are simply observations of the nature of things.

The grade of initiate is often divided into stages corresponding to the four elements, to each of which certain experiences and powers belong, but for all practical purposes the work of these subdivisions is so inter-connected that it cannot be separated. Briefly it may be said that the initiate in his progress through what are somewhat misleadingly called the Elemental Grades has to learn to use certain powers that are latent in his soul; these powers may be classed under the two heads of psychism and magic.

But again the terms are misleading, for the popular understanding of them gives little guide to their real nature. Psychism as understood by the initiate includes several technical methods for inducing the different types of extended consciousness, and concerns, among other things, divination in all its branches. Magic, on the other hand, is a much simpler and less formidable thing than popular imagination believes it to be, and is a technique for the utilisation and direction of the astral forces, which are the immediate causes behind the world of appearances. Neither of these powers are spiritual in their nature, and they are neither good nor bad save as they are used, but in dedicated hands they are enormously potent for good, for the healing of body and soul, and for regeneration, not only of individuals, but of races.

Having acquired the mastery of these powers, which is based upon self-mastery, the initiate may be deemed an adept, whether that grade be conferred symbolically or not. As an adept he learns to contact the great cosmic forces which are spiritual in their nature, and are as far superior to the astral plane as the astral plane is superior to the physical plane. Many people, from a mistaken idealism, try to by-pass the astral plane and make immediate contact with the spiritual; this, however, is not a practical proceeding and results in that confusion and incoordination so often seen in mystics. It is only by a proper technique of the astral plane that balance and co-ordination can be maintained in psychic matters, and to this end there is no adequate substitute for the magical technique.

And now, at last, we are in a position to understand the nature of those we have termed the Masters. They are nothing more or less than adepts made perfect, no longer needing to incarnate in matter, but functioning as discarnate entities on the Inner Planes. They are divided, according to tradition, into the Greater and Lesser Masters, the Greater Masters being those who passed through adepthood in civilisations earlier than our own. According to tradition, the Greater Masters incarnate upon rare occasions and for special purposes; and are known to tradition as culture-gods, civilising those they come to; the Lesser Masters incarnate more frequently, and are spoken of among initiates as the Exempt Adepts - exempt because they are free from the Wheel of Birth and Death and incarnate voluntarily and not under bondage of Karma; and adept, not Master, because they are in the body and therefore subject to the limitations of the flesh.

Those who are freed from the bondage of re-birth, having worked out all their Karma, can go on and up the stages of evolution that take place on the Inner Planes; but not all choose to do so; there are some who, renouncing heavenly bliss or Nirvana, elect to remain within call of earth in order to continue the work of service and instruction that had occupied them during their incarnate lives of adepthood.

Now it will be realised by those who have studied the preceding pages wherein is given an account of the training and making of initiates and adepts, that they are trained in the technical use of symbol-systems which enable minds accustomed to think in concrete images to realise abstractions. Those on the physical plane who want to contact the Abstract make use of a symbol-system; those in the Abstract who want to get into touch with those on this plane of concrete thinking also make us of symbol-systems as being the only means of establishing communication. When a person has reached the point where he can apprehend intuitively and do his thinking abstractly, he can dispense with symbols; but until that stage is reached, symbol-systems are indispensable, both to him, to enable him to think about abstract things at all, and to those whose way of thinking is abstract, who wish to get into touch with him. It will be seen from this that in our communications with beings on the Inner Planes we are limited to those whose language we can speak, or who can speak ours.

When a Master wishes to get into touch with the plane of form or physical plane, he, an abstract being, has to build himself a concrete form in order to communicate, and this is done on the Astral Plane out of astral substance, or as it is sometimes called, the Astral Light. Such a form is constructed in exactly the same way as the magician constructs the magical images in the Astral Light - by building them mentally in the imagination. The Master imagines himself as he was in one of his incarnations, usually the last, and the adept can either imagine himself in his astral body, and so meet the Master face to face, or, if he is psychic, pick up the Master's thought telepathically. For all practical purposes one is limited to communication with Masters of one's own Tradition until one passes beyond the need of symbols for one's abstract thinking, because it is a particular symbol-system that acts as the means of communication. These symbols, however, are not spelt out like the Morse code, but are translated in the subconscious mind into a vision of sight and hearing exactly like human life save that it is subjectively perceived as a kind of rational dream. It is obvious, therefore, how easily hallucination can arise, and how great is the need for careful and prolonged trained and experienced guidance. In fact, there is no guarantee against hallucination save what is afforded by experience, judgement and integrity.

Let us now consider the relationship between the Masters and the Orders to which they belong and in which, as men, they received their training. Upon the Inner Planes, in their own sphere, they are members of a single body, sometimes called the Great White Lodge, sometimes called the Collegium Spiritum Sanctum, or College of the Adepti; these temples are not made with hands and have no physical abiding place, but are eternal in the heavens. In their relations with the outer world, however, the Masters appear to work through and by means of the Orders to which they belong. These Orders, again, do not exist on the material plane, but on the astral, but they have their points of contact in the various Fraternities, groups gathered around an individual adept or initiate, and the various solitary and independent workers who have succeeded in "tuning-in" on their wave-length psychically.

The function of the Masters in connection with the occult schools is all-important; in fact one might say that it is they who really constitute the school. Their relation to it is similar to that of the senate of a university; they are the governing body; they alone have the power to grant degrees, and some, though not all, may take part in the actual teaching.

The manner in which the Masters teach, however, is different from the methods used by mundane teachers; for the most part they do not give personal instruction to individual pupils, but focus and transmit powerful psychic influences, and, as it were, stand behind the adepti engaged in the work of the school. These psychic influences play a most important part in the training of initiates. The doctrines of the occult Orders can be got from books, and so can their methods by those who have had some practical experience in psychic matters and can read between the lines; but this concentrated psychic influence, this peculiar driving-power, is an altogether different matter, is something quite unique, and has to be experienced in order to be realised.

This psychic influence is the real motive power of an occult fraternity, and its presence or absence determines its power to initiate. We have never stressed this aspect in the Fraternity of the Inner Light, leaving it to be inferred; but now that the development of the work of the Fraternity makes it necessary to delegate so much of it, and that a generation of members has arisen who are not my students, but the students of my students, I think it as well to make this information known for their guidance; for the first intimations of this influence are so subtle that they may pass unnoticed, their significance not being realised, unless it is known that they are to be expected, and are an integral part of the training that is given in this Fraternity.

Teachings of the Masters

Dion Fortune had been forging her own contacts with the Masters since 1921 and some of her close associates over the years were also trained in this facility. A body of teaching was thus built up from various Masters, a selection from which we give here as demonstration of the range of their activities and interests.

The first is from the one largely responsible for helping Dion Fortune to found her fraternity, who is sometimes referred to as "the English Master", although there is probably more than one who could validly lay claim to such a title or description. In the extract we choose he is speaking upon the subject of Masters.

There are a number of beings on the inner planes who have come through "the rounds of humanity" and who have no need to enter into incarnation again. Some of these you call "Masters" but there are really many grades of them so that the all-inclusive term "Inner Plane Adepti" is possibly a wiser expression.

The beings of whom I am going to speak are all human. I shall not speak of certain very remote Guides who are not men and never have been. The Inner Plane Adeptus of the human kind has come through many incarnations until it is no longer necessary for his further development to continue living the earth life. Therefore according to their grades and their particular esoteric needs such either retire to very far off spheres or they remain not indeed on Earth but within touch of it.

How do they keep in touch with it? They do so by a very remarkable and age long developed system of telepathy which flashes a message into the consciousnesses of many people on Earth or, in the case of "mediums," can send a message in a continuous flow and keep the whole contact near the Earth for a certain time.

As I have said, there are many grades among the Inner Plane Adepti and you must realise that all of them, though they have no further need for Earth lessons obtained through incarnation, still have need of evolving themselves in different ways and on other planes. There are very many forms of development for them which I cannot dwell upon now but, broadly speaking, they may be counted as a kind of planetary initiation beyond the Earth; there are several such. According to the inner plane initiation which a Master has taken, so is his esoteric grade - the initiations of occult groups in the world are shadows of these things but there is a certain likeness.

Those among the Masters - I use the word "Masters" here deliberately - who have reached a certain grade on the inner planes then occupy themselves not only with the general helping of humanity but also with a special work connected with the forces behind evolution as they show themselves in different countries. Such Masters have, as it were, areas of national force allotted to them; sometimes a whole continent is allotted to one for his particular sphere of work. This work naturally varies with the type of force of the Master, and certainly some Masters are concerned with working upon evolution through special teaching of their Order and bringing such teaching down to groups.

As those in touch with the Inner Plane Adepti proceed in their evolution they are given certain work to do for themselves and by that work they themselves continue to learn by degrees. Such work given to a pupil by an Inner Plane Adeptus might not always sound very interesting to you but the pupil has to begin with small matters. He may be called upon to take a message to someone in trouble or to put some man or woman in the world in touch with his own contact. Very often such people who are given lesser tasks like this are permanently on the inner planes; they are known as "guides" but they must not be confused with the various types of human beings known as "guides" by the spiritualists. The occult "guide" on the inner planes is usually entrusted with certain pupils, to help them and report on them and watch carefully over what they do.

As you well know, there is a great difference between Eastern and Western teaching on this subject as it is necessary to work according to the conditions in that part of the world where the work is being done. In the hurry of modern life with its increasing mechanisation and the general noise and bustle, force cannot be concentrated in the West as easily as it can in the East, nor are the bodies of western men fitted for what I would call a constant in and out going of the physical body, and this makes it difficult to concentrate force today in the West. For that reason rituals have been made to concentrate power in certain tracks and bring it down in that way. All this you know but it is useful to repeat it.

an English Master

The difference between eastern and western esoteric traditions, here mentioned, has been touched on by other Masters. The following passage is from one who is particularly concerned with 'the beginnings of things' which includes both early Christianity and the spiritualist movement.

There is a very good example in the Theosophical Society of how many eastern teachings came back to the West and set fire anew to western occultism. First of all it was essential to wake up the ordinary Victorian rather dull, respectable, unimaginative classes who had, speaking generally, no particular faith in the Protestant forms they practised - the Catholics were always in another category. These people who had no special faith did not believe at all in continuity of life after the body fell into ashes and ceased to be. Therefore that side of things had somehow to be awoken in them. For that cause there was a movement known as Spiritualism set afoot, by which through mediums these people could get into touch with their departed friends, so that they could make for the first time some sort of contact with the inner planes which they were able to believe with the conscious mind. It does not matter that the movement was often associated with the uneducated and even foolishly sentimental, as well indeed, as with a few very intelligent persons; the point is that in order to investigate this movement, accounted foolish and ignorant and a channel of fraud, persons in authority went out to investigate these matters and found the Inner Plane Adepti and those of higher grade and of different teaching. Therefore was the Theosophical Society begun and therefore through Spiritualism, in spite of the contempt of many for it, this meeting of East and West took place, and the great inner plane forces began to penetrate all over the world into the mundane minds of ordinary people.

Hilarion

Another Master of some repute takes up the subject of East and West as follows. He is one who is credited in some circles with holding the inner office of Lord of Civilisation, which might loosely be interpreted as a kind of General Secretary of an interior United Nations, although all such analogies are somewhat limited, to the point of distortion, by the very different perspective of those who are limited by earthly consciousness and those who are not. However, it is sometimes necessary to make these rough comparisons, in order that any approach to understanding may be achieved at all.

The subject on which I am going to speak to you tonight may not seem at first particularly important but it is one that has profound implications in the Aquarian Age; probably much that I will say will not be new to you but it is a subject that I myself am very much engaged upon and one which it is very necessary should be brought to the fore in your consciousness. This subject concerns the affinities between the Eastern and Western Traditions. The reason I am particularly concerned is that it is a matter that greatly affects the work of the Hierarchy within Racial Spirits and Souls and Group life, and the relations between different nations. It is now indeed a very complex matter.

You may or may not have realised that the time has now been reached when there is no 'Eastern Tradition' or 'Western Tradition' but only the one 'Tradition'; for sufficient work has been done by those of the Eastern Mysteries and those on the Western Path to enable a strong link to have been forged, and now there is one clear Path. That, of course, is speaking in the archetypal sense - the Path is by no means clear in manifestation and has, in fact, to be worked upon and gradually made clearer by all concerned. Of course the ideals behind the Eastern and Western Traditions are the same; the emphasis in each Path has been concerned with the particular task in hand and the levels on which the work was carried out. It will be found that when the Traditions are examined on their own levels there is no opposition or differences, but confusion has arisen when methods of one which are worked out for the one are taken out of their proper environment and used on levels on which they were not intended to be used.

This matter of the *one* Tradition, this matter of the affinities between the Eastern Tradition and the Western Tradition is one on which you who are in incarnation must really work especially hard, for the problems are mainly on your plane. They do not penetrate to the planes on which the Masters work. Do not think by this we are unaware of or unaffected by this; on the contrary, we are aware and affected and we do all we can to help in such things, many great souls incarnating especially to concentrate on this matter - but the working out of these things can only be done by those on the physical plane.

You will find hidden in the records of the Eastern and the Western Traditions the same wisdom, the same profound psychological insight into man's nature, the same capacity for, and use of, magical powers; the only difference is in the technique employed, the symbolism and language used and the way different levels are worked. Much good work has in fact been done by western scholars bringing illumination to the West through the study of eastern works; in another way much has been done for the Eastern Tradition on the lower levels through the practical application of the Western Tradition. It is because men do not realise the affinity of the Traditions and that the time has now come that the one Path has opened up, that much confusion and tragedy and unfortunately ill repute for both Traditions has occurred among ill informed people - especially when mistakes are made.

The Masters of both Traditions now work almost anywhere, no longer conditioned by the Traditions, and the teaching which is coming through from eastern Masters in western groups is in terms of the modern western needs, and the same is happening in regard to many western Masters who are helping in regard to eastern souls. I myself am one who works with both, although to the Masters who have gone sufficiently far there is no difference and only one Tradition - for all lead the same way toward the Light. The ideals and aspiration may open the door to any aspect of the Path.

At this time in your national life there is great need for the inoculation of esoteric Christianity. It is in the affinity between that teaching and the wisdom of the Eastern Tradition on the more abstract levels that the hope of the world for a more noble life lies. On this note I will close.

Rakoczi

A practical example of this affinity between Eastern and Western traditions was exemplified at one of the Society's discussion groups that was studying *"The Rays and the Initiations"* by Alice A. Bailey, the amenuensis of one known as the Tibetan Master. To clairvoyant sight "a figure from a remote distance wearing strange Tibetan or semi-Mongolian robes and head dress came down a slanting beam of blue light, bearing bread and wine." The following day he put through the following message:

I want you to be clear about the teaching which is all in the book. I sent through a contact last night which I think was perceived under the symbols of the bread and wine. In various ways these symbols, both pure and debased, can be found underlying the structure of the Western Mysteries. The Church has fought over their Christian significance - as to whether the meaning is commemorative or magical or both - but their full significance will not be realised until the Kingdom comes.

I yearn upon the West, but it must be brought to fruition in its own way and at its own time; its abilities are not like our own. Bread and wine are symbols of the Creative Word - thus when Christ replied in answer to the taunt "Command these stones to be made bread": "not by bread alone does man live but in every Word which proceedeth out of the Mouth of God," he uttered a profound esoteric truth which has never been enough thought upon.

Djwal Khul

As Dion Fortune has pointed out in her remarks upon other "inhabitants of the Unseen" there are other beings beside the human which we need to be aware of beyond the bounds of fairy tales and popular superstition. These are the inhabitants of the Elemental Kingdoms in whose life we all share, as a perfectly natural part of life, and in which the human being has a particular responsibility in participating also in the life of the Spirit. By this means are both human and Elemental raised up in the Great Work of spiritual evolution, about which one Master particularly concerned with such contacts had this to say:

Beauty and power are the keynotes of the Elemental Kingdom with which I am associated in my work, because I work both with the Elemental Kingdom and in it. They are, in a sense, both the tools I use, and also the media in which I work - just as a man can say, direct a jet of water from a hose, or also, as a diver, carry on his business in the depths of the ocean. You all must learn to do the same with your Personalities; they are tools to be used and perfected as a scientist perfects his instruments, but to the artist they are the very substance of his self expression, and these two aspects should ever work together in the Great Work.

Your Personalities, compounded of the four Elemental essences, form a chalice for the indwelling Spirit. That was the original Plan and toward that Plan we work, but alas, as things are, some Personalities are unaware of or refuse to recognise the reason for their being and their true function. The Personality should express itself in the world around it - in its environment - but should draw its life from the indwelling Spirit else it is driven by the conflicting forces which are around it and within it due to its karmic past and the karma of the human race. All practical treatises on occult matters and all religions try, in essence, to tell how to re-form the link between the Personality and the Spirit. For without this link the Personality merely goes round and round in its own circle, hence the saying that no man may lift himself by his own shoe strings. That is true as far as it goes, but man is much more than is generally realised and that unrealised part *can* draw upwards. Faith is the necessary framework for the building of this bridge because faith connects the Personality with the Supernals where dwells man's Spirit. That faith, which is something which transcends the concrete mind is of the nature of the Supernals - it is not part of the Personality although it can be experienced by the Personality.

Let us examine more closely how we can bring about this fuller integration which is necessary before the destiny of man can fulfil itself and before he can take his full share in the Great Work. It has been said that wishing and willing help in progressing. Is that not another way of saying that there must first be the desire held? And that means that there is a goal envisaged (even though it may be a nameless one) or there would be no desire; that is the first stage. The second stage - the willing - is an attribute of the Spirit which *has* power and *can* obtain its goals because its goals are in line with the Logoidal Will and therefore there is no barrier. And the willing requires that faith which knows that it can bring about what it wills. There you have already formed some linkage or bridge between the Personality and the Spirit because the desire for the goal is something experienced by the Personality even though it may be reactions to influences pressing down upon it from the inner planes from its own Essential Self. So it then looks upward, as it were, and desires - and despise not desire, my brethren, for the strength of the Personality arises from its depths and desire is the great driving force of the Personality nature. So it looks upward and desires, and then it has the faith that its real self not only can but will bring about the goal, though the goal is nameless. The Personality cannot give a name to what it seeks for what it seeks is above form and so, to the Personality, is unknown. It is as if the goal were the Unknown God to the lower self.

All the forces of the Elements are necessary in this quest. The freedom of Air. The adaptability which accepts changed attitudes, which is of Water. The driving force of Fire and the ability to destroy and permit destruction in order that something better may come. And the endurance and strength of Earth to remain steadfast in the Quest for ever, for he who will endure to the end will receive all things.

Serapis

Forming a pathway between Spirit and Personality is sometimes called building the Rainbow Bridge and in its initial stages at least, the building blocks from which such a bridge is formed consist of various forms of symbolism.. A Master associated with the traditions of that great store house of deep symbolism, ancient Egypt, has advice to give on this score.

Since you are in the world, do not hesitate to avail yourselves of all the help that symbols can give you. The use of colour, the steeping yourselves in suitable atmospheres through reading, and when opportunity permits, the steeping yourselves in atmospheres to be found in Nature's surroundings or music and the beauty created through the arts. Avail yourselves of all these opportunities; but, having availed yourselves of the opportunities, see that you carry the work through and use the force.

I cannot overstress the importance of this *use*. So much in the national life is wrong, not because of the lack of anything but because on the one hand there are those who do not know and therefore do not use the opportunities of life, and on the other hand there are those who abuse the opportunities of life.

Astrological symbols are a very potent means of linking the mind up with fundamental principles, for they are very old indeed and were used when men used not so much the conscious mind mentation, but the subconscious mind mentation; they appeal to the imagination and open up the subconscious. If you will meditate upon them and once get an idea you will find that you will be able to go on almost endlessly with the correspondences that will well up from the deeps of the subconscious. They were used as symbols when men could not read or reason, but they taught, and they taught not through the reasoning power, but through an awareness of the principles which they illustrated. There is much power connected with these symbols as you can find out for yourselves by building them up in your imagination and meditating upon them.

I would ask you to dwell much upon the concept of the whole, for in these days of specialisation and the separateness they induce, there is much danger of disintegration. We see reflected in the world today this lack of understanding of the right relationship of the whole, and unless this realisation of the unity of the whole is brought home to men's minds much suffering will ensue.

Always remember that in the centre of the universe, within the centre of your own being, there is a Central Stillness where all is harmony, and you can ever draw upon this to help you to the realisation of that right relationship of the various aspects of life, both objectively and subjectively.

an Egyptian Master

One early contact of Dion Fortune's mediumship resulted in a book full of cosmic symbolism which was subsequently published as "The Cosmic Doctrine". The Master concerned also gave other instruction from time to time, often of a very practical nature, including this description of the after death condition.

I am known, I think, before anything else, as a teacher. Have you ever deeply considered what real teaching is, or rather, what it ought to be? When you reach the invisible planes you will find, according to your degree of development, a curious condition which makes it appear that instead of looking at things from outside, as has been your normal custom in the world you have left, you will find that all things are in you. You will therefore examine those things within yourself, for they are there, instead of looking at them through the lens of some friend's personality or through the physical eyes as you did on the plane of the visible world.

Now think for a moment what this means. You regard all things within yourself. You wish to find out about something and you look at it within yourself - not, as you have considered it, outside yourself. According to your development will you be able to hold within you the greatest possibilities of viewing things in yourself; and you will get, obviously, a deeper knowledge by looking at them from such an intimate and unusual and close point of view.

I said, "according to your development." It is because of this fact that many souls who have passed out of the world phase onto the inner planes, when the people in the visible world are sometimes able to contact them, they contact what appears to be a form of clairvoyance, greater or lesser according to the type and development of the invisible communicator. Such a person, such a communicator from the invisible world, need not have been what is called a clairvoyant in outer life, but by his new faculty of being able to realise far more within himself, even of matters referring to people and to countries at a distance, he may appear to you what is called clairvoyant.

It is on this fact that the assumption has been built that those who are "dead", as it is called, may give some account of future events to the living. And it is true up to a point that they can give some account according to their own development and according to the type of contact, and the purity of the contact between the one on the visible plane and the communicator on the invisible planes. When, however, the communicating being on the inner planes is of a very much greater condition of intelligence and spiritual dedication, when, in short, he is what you call one of the Inner Plane Adepti, you may conceive to some extent the tremendous amount of matters he holds in contemplation within himself - far, far more than the ordinary soul, however well meaning, who passes over into the invisible world. That is why, speaking as a general fact, communication with an Inner Plane Adept, or those of his pupils trained by him on the inner planes, bears so much more fruit than can ever be found by contacting the countless well meaning intelligence and desire to help of one only developed on the same level as most men are, or very little beyond.

In short, that is the main difference between the reasons for contacting and learning from one of yourselves, little more developed than you are, which is called spiritualism. I am not particularly against this latter type of communication, save only to remark that it does harm to such a communicator to be kept constantly in touch with the Earth. And unless or until a special message he may deeply wish, and possibly be ordered to give to the world, has been given, you should not hurt your friend's development too much by constantly calling on him for help and for the ironing out of small problems, any more than, for different reasons, you should contact the Masters merely for help in small mundane plane matters which you on this plane are meant to solve for yourselves; unless indeed it is a matter which is not ordinary and where real help is necessary - then you may be assured that if you ask for that help you will get it.

a Greek Master

Contacts with David Carstairs

As we have seen, it was some years before Dion Fortune came out into the open and admitted the fact of her personal contact with the Masters. Other occultists have shown even more reserve. MacGregor Mathers of the Golden Dawn preferred simply to refer vaguely to Secret Chiefs without mentioning any names or specific contacts. In some respects this might be considered a wise policy considering the problems that beset Madame Blavatsky in controversies about the alleged status and genuineness of her Masters. Nonetheless it seems a dire judgement upon human affairs if the truth may not be spoken for fear of its being distorted or misunderstood.

This problem also concerns the naming of Masters. Obviously some name or means of identity is required as a basic requirement for any communication between the planes. The trouble is that when such an identity coincides with that of a known historical personage all kinds of misunderstandings are likely to arise.

As has been revealed in at least one biography of Dion Fortune her principal contact of this nature was variously identified with a former Lord Chancellor, of whom there are three candidates, all with Christian names of Thomas, Thomas Erskine, Thomas More and Thomas á Becket. Whether one wishes to treat these identifications as symbolic or real or illusory or simply flags of convenience is a free choice. The crux of the matter for any occultist of experience is the quality of any such communication rather than its alleged source.

In the context of the possible interface between spiritualism and occultism it is interesting to turn to early records of Dion Fortune's mediumistic contacts, which seem to be very much in the nature of a spiritualist type of contact, particularly in the case of one who announces himself as David Carstairs, killed at Ypres in the Great War. As it turns out, he seems to be rather more than a recent casualty of war seeking companionship or guidance, for he becomes the intermediary and introductor to a range of higher contacts, the Masters who communicated with Dion Fortune for the rest of her life.

These few extracts from early trance contacts give something of the ambience of the psychic experiments of Violet M. Firth, as she then was, at Glastonbury in the company of her early friend and colleague C.T. Loveday, and a variety of other occasional participants, which included Frederick Bligh Bond, the archaeological investigator of Glastonbury Abbey by psychic means.

Here is one of 10th November 1922 where Carstairs talks a little about himself, plainly in answer to a question:

Do I know the name Carstairs? Ought to. Signed cheques with it. My father was a cycle manufacturer in Coventry. I couldn't get on with office work. I was in the Cycle Corps. Of course I am pretty close to the Earth. Haven't been over very long. That is why I was put on this job. Makes it easier. The others have been dead a long time. Lucky to get the job, wasn't I?

A couple of weeks later, on 28th November 1922, it seems that they offer to try to make contact with his family, but he declines the offer.

No, nothing personal. I have no personality. Things in the Midlands are best left. I am obliged, all the same. There was enough trouble over me in life. I don't want to poke my nose in, no one has asked after me. You cannot wait for people when evolution is on the march, have to keep up with your regiment.

He went on in this and subsequent talks to give a range of teaching of a general occult nature off his own bat, rather after the fashion of the teaching kind of spiritualist guide. He makes reference to this on 13th December 1922, along with one or two self revelatory remarks.

So you have been giving yourselves a holiday. Might have asked me. I'd have sat on your knee - gone half price.

How are you getting on with my words of wisdom? You'll have to edit me. "I ain't no scholar." I was fond of learning, but had no polish - no university stunt. They smacked me through school. Thought that was enough. Got me in the office. Thought me an awful nuisance though I was harmless. Could not drive a bargain nor men. Let the pater in for bad contracts. Said I must be fired.

Then I got "lung-ed" and the Doctor fired me instead. I liked the scouts better than the pater's beastly work. I was an authority on ash buckets in our town. Brought infant mortality down. Where there is dirt there are flies and dead babies. Be one here if you don't clean up."

And some fifteen months, on 27th February 1924, before he takes up the personal theme again, almost as an aside, possibly in response to a couple of guests being present, one of them Netta Fornario, who had apparently just written an autobiographical work of her own: "Interpretation" under her pen name of Mack Tyler.

Did I ever tell you my story? You got some bits. I was nobody in particular. Mater honest, but not poor. I was eldest of five. Three boys, two girls. I didn't do well in business. That annoyed the Pater. He wondered whether it was cheaper to pay me a salary or a pension. I wanted the salary you see I got my eye on a girl. I should have retired earlier otherwise. Like most of us, we find girls a problem. I was puzzled because I got T.B. Had it in my knee and hip, but got over it. In splints till I was eight. Thought she would have me. Asked the Pater what he thought of it. Told him I was thinking of getting spliced, was it alright? You and Mother are all sound, I was the only crock in the family. Pater turned pea-green, said "Afraid it isn't alright. The four aren't your brothers and sisters, they are only half-brothers and sisters. Your mother died two weeks after you were born, of T.B. I'd cut my throat before I'd do the same again." So I cut it. Then I took up the Boy Scouts. If I couldn't have a family in one way I thought I'd have one in another. Then it started in my lungs again, and Pater said he'd pension me.

One day I said "Pater, you are a grandfather." I had 28 at a birth, and showed him my first troop. He bought the layette, and was very pleased. That's how we got the organisation going.

I organised it partly on a big scale. It spread, and various folk helped me. My best girl got a bit left. Then she took it on and got 15 at a birth - all girls. Then we organised our District for a rally. She for the girls, I for the boys. She organised her District, and I the lot. Then I got a pal, and put them to work together. They soon got engaged and married.

In the course of this period he had also introduced other inner plane contacts, after the manner of a spiritualist control. Two of these were these were to play a major role in Dion Fortune's life's work, one, usually called "the Greek" or even "the old Greek" being responsible for dictating much of "The Cosmic Doctrine", the other, referred to as "Lord E." was her constant inner companion and mentor for the rest of her life in the building and maintaining of her Fraternity.

Some of the difficulties involved in starting up this kind of project, as seen from the inner side, are mentioned from time to time.

Well, how are you getting on with the new teacher? He is finished for tonight. He does not find it easy to do yet. He has been over a long time. He was a Greek. Yes, the one mentioned before. He is working from a pretty high plane, and the result is that the vibrations get a bit faint. Not like me; just next door. He may be a bit scrappy, it will want sorting out. He is fond of aphorisms.

Lord E. was unusually good. He was used to public speaking. This man is more used to dealing with pupils by question and answer, as they did in Greece. He would get on the step of some public building, and young men would come and ask how many eggs made five, and he would tell them. He was later than Pythagoras. He got put to death, was a bit too much for them.

He finds it hard to keep a contact at all. He has to come down a plane as we have to go up one. He isn't working from his own plane, but from the one below, and to do that he has to construct a vehicle, two moves, as it were. He is on the 5th plane, as is Lord E. This one is not so good in coming down. I work from the plane on which I live - the 4th - they use me because I can get through easily.

You have a 4th plane medium. Most are of the 3rd plane. This one can be got on to the 5th if necessary, which is very rare. If you hoist her on to the 5th plane a 6th plane Master can come down, and this is how initiations were done.

Now at one time it was as much fuss to get her on to the 4th plane as it is now to the 5th, but now she can come and go as she likes on the 4th, but we have to hoist her on to the 5th.

You are ahead of your schedule on this work. We did not expect to start this till after Christmas, but all goes very smoothly. It is quite unusual to work a medium as much as this.

By 31st December 1922 another communicator had been introduced to help put through "The Cosmic Doctrine", whose identity is not given. However Carstairs has this to say about him.

You will find the new man easier than the Greek. He will be with you from time to time. He was a great educationist in his day. They are always easier when used to lecturing. It is just as hard to get a person to telepath on our side as to receive on yours, and they vary just as much. You should pump the Greek with questions. He knows a lot, not like me.

Some of the communicators are pretty highly placed and it is a job for them to get through at all. The higher things can only be given in scraps and aphorisms. They can't transmit a connected lecture from that plane. But you will find you will get a lot by asking questions. The more you ask the more you get. When we lecture we are pushing from our end, and when you ask you are pulling from your end. You'll get a regular hotchpotch of scraps given you and you will sort them out and get them into subjects, and all the matter relating to one subject in one place - enough cross references to fill a volume. You will see when you get to your index.

And so things continued and developed on a fairly informal basis until the time came when it was plainly stated by Carstairs, in a question and answer question with "Merl", Dr. Penry Evans, whom Dion Fortune married in 1927.

DC: Now do you see what these chaps are driving at?
M: To establish a school on a basis of discipline.
DC: And they don't want molly-coddles. If you can't stand a hammering, go home, see? It is not a bit of use pretending it is a bed of roses; it isn't. There is a great deal of difference between half-ideals and true ideals. But we are not out for those short cuts to comfort. We are out for something much bigger than that. You can't say where it begins or ends.

On the 22nd June 1928, the Summer Solstice of that year, this statement was ratified with the confirmation of the nature of the work that lay ahead in the establishment of an occult Fraternity with headquarters in both Glastonbury and London.

You have got your foundations in now. That is what all the preliminary work has been. The worst of your troubles are behind you, and the interesting parts are beginning. You are beginning to see the fruits of your labours. You have got to about the end of your first stage.

You will find that trance will take on a secondary position and ritual is the thing. It means instead of one person doing a stunt, the whole lot will do a stunt. Don't you see what happens in ritual? The whole team shifts consciousness. That's the game.

The dynamics and motivation of ritual are not the subject of this book, for which see our companion volume "An Introduction to Ritual Magic" where David Carstairs also figures, seventy years later.

There has been speculation, as in one biography of Dion Fortune, as to whether David Carstairs ever really did exist. There is no record of an officer of that name, although if he was brought up by foster parents we cannot be sure by what name he may have enlisted.

Whatever the truth in this matter a character very much like him has continued to make contact over the years, and concerned with much the same things. One important contact came on the anniversary of Armistice Day, November 11th 1957 in a trance address to senior members of the Fraternity. The medium of course was no longer Dion Fortune, who had departed this life some eleven years previously. It is interesting not only from the point of view of his own long term concern with war and its effects, but also on post mortem conditions generally, to say nothing of Group and National Angels.

There appears to be some confusion of terminology as to "traitors" or "war criminals" - possibly with his wider viewpoint "traitors to the human race" may have been in mind - but the application of his remarks is clear.

It is a very long time since I last spoke to you here and there are many whom I do not know, but I see several that I remember well and to them I do give a particular greeting.

I want to talk tonight about the esoteric conditions brought about by war. Since I have been in this present stage of existence on the inner planes I have been able to notice very many conditions which I think we do not recognise much on the mundane plane in ordinary life. There is much about death in war which can probably be told you far more fully by the ordinary spiritualistic séance, but you will not be particularly interested in that side. Generally speaking, the thing that you notice most is how a human being's attitude and belief does continue influencing him for some time, probably for many, many years after the body dies. If the human being has no specific belief in an after life (as you call it) or in his own eternal spirit and the spirits of other people, too, he goes into a species of coma - a coma not quite like what you call a coma in the world. He passes into that state and he really has no particular consciousness, perhaps for years.

When I came over and saw the various conditions on the inner planes left by war, I felt that I wanted to devote myself to the state of men after war so far as I was able, not only to help those who actually died in battle, but to help those who took part in various movements often called treason and which involved judicial execution. To those unfortunate human beings I have endeavoured to give such help as was possible, and some of the greatest difficulties in these cases was with the Germans, because, although there are many Germans who have a special belief in after life there are very, very many who believe in nothing at all and who feel that the death of the body is the end. And therefore, I was unable to do very much for Germans in those cases; but I did attend the Nuremberg trials. I did wait for those who were sent on to this plane afterwards, and others with me, also, did what we could. And here is a very strange thing: you have to forget any patriotic feelings you may have had in the world. You find you are thinking of humanity as a whole, and the thing you judge by is the condition of the spirit of the traitor, if you like I will use that word, the spirit of the traitor himself, for sometimes though he may be, from your point of view, deeply misguided and wrong, to say no worse, he has really followed the light within him right up to the time, probably, of his condemnation and subsequent execution - and those executions, remember, are not pretty or pleasant either to suffer or to see. But where you find there has been a true call from the traitor's Higher Self to do certain deeds which have got him into such a bad state in the world, you can always help that man or woman afterwards, though it is easier where there is some kind of religious belief, no matter what the Church or creed; an orthodox Jew, if you like, or a Roman Catholic, a really believing Protestant, but some form of real belief, that does help, though it may not be much in line with your own teachings here.

You can gain yet wider understanding of war conditions when you are in my place, not only as concerns humanity but the conditions that hold humanity as it were in their various hives or shells, conditions you would call those that belong to the Racial Soul, and certain yet wider and yet farther off things which belong to the Racial Angel and his dominion. And I think, myself, that the reason why the Germans have been so difficult to understand and why they have lost their heads so often has been that they have no proper guiding Racial Spirit. The guiding Spirit has been the mind of man, to be precise, of Bismark long ago, and that mind of man welded together, indeed, the little German Group Souls of many areas, but the whole country, though it counted as an Empire, was not an Empire under a great guiding Angel as were the old consolidated kingdoms such as France, England and others.

The curious tensions of the various parts of the esoteric side of this planet work very strongly in conditions of war, and you cannot help being aware of this here, though it is difficult to explain it in a very clear way. When there is multitudinous death for any reason, either a widespread epidemic, such as the Black Death, or wholesale war such as we have twice had in this century, you get two very strong and opposing influences. One is the tremendous amount of decaying substance - I am sorry to be unpleasant - which is added to the earth which can attract very bad conditions, and thus bad entities. The other is a tremendous band of ever swelling etheric forces when it is a case of the dead who have died in war. That great etheric band is swelled by a huge mass of youth, remember, a tremendous amount of courage, aspiration, and various other emotions, and that condition is in itself a great power, for it is in that etheric state produced through this multitudinous death that the form of the new ways of life begin to come through and begin to gather force, to enter again the arena of the world itself on its outer planes, and as so many too fondly hoped, make a new world.

Now this happened to a very large extent after the First World War. Some of you may remember that it was supposed to be a "war to end war". Alas, I doubt if such a war will ever be on this planet, a war to end war, until human beings themselves are utterly and entirely different; but there are two interesting esoteric facts I would speak of. The First World War, some of you may remember, brought through great phases of influence in the arts. Many soldiers were poets and musicians, and some of them even contrived to continue being so, almost on the battlefield - not just two or three romantic young men, but quite a large percentage of soldiers and servicemen of all kinds. There was a tremendous influx of that great power that roughly we call art, and it worked through the arts; not only that, but the very forms of war became, in a sense, new forms of art. Perception was able to be used under the water and up in the air. That made a great deal of difference to one's understanding of perception. And yet another thing, that First World War was the end, the actual breaking up of the Piscean Age, in a practical sense. It absolutely finished it. Nothing could be the same again.

Then came the armistice for some years, for that is all you can call it. The Second World War was only a continuation of the First after a break; and here in this second war quite other conditions came about. I do not say that people were any the less self-sacrificing or brave, and they went through horrors, possibly worse, certainly as bad, but the attitude of all was different. They started tired in spirit, they started with no sort of romantic ideal behind, and the force that came through with the vast amount of trouble, death and suffering was a force which lent itself to science, to scientific discoveries of all sorts, very valuable and very interesting. That is what the etheric power loosened by the dead of the Second World War has given you. And the mind of man has also loosened up a great deal from all the instability of the world. The orthodox Churches may not, indeed, close, but they lose yet more of their influence, and the ordinary "man in the street" tends to believe either in Spiritualism or in some form of occultism, or in some finding that he can get through the various psychological teachings there are; but less and less can he accept the old fashioned dogmas. I am talking in a general sense.

These are thoughts I think which can very well fill our minds on Armistice Day; and these great forms, remember, which you find of great service and interest today, have been in an indirect way brought about by life itself offered up in a special way to the country. So think of that.

The other point I would like to speak about is the Racial Angel. There is, of course, in all the old nations that particular Group Being, or Spirit, at the head of all. He is, really, one of the Lords of

Flame, for they became National Angels; and with certain nations there is a great impact of that Angel. With other nations the Angel at the head is not as close in contact with the nation he rules. In Britain there is, relatively, a great deal of contact with that Angel, and the reason is - it is often said in jest on the Continent - that the English are naturally a most remarkably religious race. By "English" is meant, of course, the people of the British Isles generally. They may not follow some particular Church but their mind desires some form of religious belief and exercise, and they will have it, and that is their special weakness in certain historical matters, and partly their great strength. And more and more will it be their great strength as time goes on, for, believe me, after all we have suffered in these Wars we cannot take the same place in politics as we have taken before; we can only go in with other nations of the West as brethren and work together all we can for the general freedom - actually, as you will readily agree, a higher thing than thinking only of one's own nation all the time.

And so the Wars, terrible as they have been, have also been gates of all kinds, open gates of art and science, and, above all, of the knowledge of humanity; and that, I hope you will all think about.

That is really all I have to say on Armistice Day, but I thank you very much for listening to me patiently, and I hope I have given some sort of light shedding on the Inner Planes as Armistice Day affects them. I give then, not only my greeting, but the greeting of many hundreds who, like me, are on the inner planes through this War, and no less citizens, but citizens of Eternity. Greeting, my friends.

PART FOUR

THE PSYCHOLOGY OF PSYCHIC AND HIGHER CONSCIOUSNESS

Clairvoyance

An adequate study for the psychology of psychism is subject matter for a book. When such a study is attempted, it is immediately seen how inadequate is the average clairvoyant's explanation of his vision. He declares that he sees the presences he describes. As a matter of fact he no more sees them on the astral plane than he sees chairs and tables on the physical plane, as anyone who understands the physiology of vision is aware. He reacts to their emanations, and he reacts according to certain reaction habits, which have become stereotyped by experience. Even in the vision of the physical eye on the material plane we never "see" the object to which we react, we only feel the sensations which the reaction of the cells of the retina to the light, reflected from the object on to their surface, cause to take place among the cells of the brain. Impair the retina, the connecting nerve, or the brain cells concerned with vision, and the object disappears.

In all vision we never "see" the object, we only look into our own consciousness as the Lady of Shalott looked into the magic mirror. It is by practice and habit we learn to refer to an object to position in space and this power of judgement is the result of binocular vision. We judge distance by the angle of convergence of the focus of our two eyes. Moreover, in dealing with a familiar object we do not look at it in detail, we recognise it by a general impression of its salient features, and infer the rest.

I well remember an experience which befell me as a child, and which is very illustrative of the psychology of vision. Awakening in the dim light of dawn, I saw on the windowsill in my nursery an unfamiliar object, which appeared to me to be a large rabbit. I gazed at it enraptured till the growing light revealed it to be a little pile of clean linen. Some familiar curve of the bundle had suggested the rabbit's fat back, and my imagination had supplied the rest of its anatomy from memory.

Exactly the same mechanism is at work with the clairvoyant. Upon a newly developed sense centre in consciousness impinge vibrations of an unfamiliar character. He is receiving in a higher octave than is available for the five physical senses, he interprets the unfamiliar vibrations in the nearest stock image he has got in consciousness. He generally gets an accurate analogy; and provided it is recognised that what he interprets in terms of sense consciousness is but a symbolic representation of the psychic actuality, no harm is done. He translates his impressions back into terms of their own plane, and the result becomes clear.

Trouble arises, however, when, with what is termed naive psychology, he accepts what he perceives as being an exact portrayal of the objects represented, and concludes that the inner planes are but etherealised copies of the material planes with which his senses have made him familiar.

A little consideration will show why this is not, and cannot be, a fact. Take first the robed forms of spirits that appear to the vision of the seer. We know that they have no physical bodies, but are intelligences. Upon what, then, having no shoulder blades, do they hang their robes? We are seeing our own thought forms of what we think such presences ought to look like, and our concepts are determined by traditional religious art, which always puts its sacred figures into classical draperies. It is very interesting to note that in the visions of Asiatics, a similar conventionalising of the angelic presence occurs, which is invariably seen in terms of Oriental art. I shall always remember the gasp which the audience gave when, in the Annunciation scene in Rutland Boughton's "Bethlehem", the archangel Gabriel appeared in tunic and tights. The effect produced by the production of Shakespeare in modern dress throws a very great deal of light on the psychology of clairvoyance.

It is my contention that the clairvoyants see nothing but the reactions in their own consciousness produced by the influences impinging upon them, and that it is the translation of these impressions into the nearest equivalent image in memory which endows the angelic visitants with form and voice.

The trained occultist, properly tuning in on the planes, does not employ this visual consciousness, but perceives direct, without the need of translation from a symbolic rendering. He perceives the thought impressions of the mental plane as ideas and the forces of the astral plane as emotions. All form is subjective. It is out of this realisation that his dominion over it comes.

Accustomed to refer an object to position in space according to its size and clarity, the untrained clairvoyant does with the visual images evoked from his subconscious mind by psychic stimulus exactly the same thing that he is in the habit of doing with the visual images evoked by the stimulation of his retina. In the language of psychology, he "projects" them. It is the same mechanism, which occurs when the lunatic, having good cause for self-reproach, refuses to recognise his memories as concerning himself, and "hears" the voice of a demon shouting abuse at him from the picture rail.

In the case of the lunatic it is recognised that a dissociation of personality has occurred, and that the mind is no longer being held together by the unifying ego. A part has got into a state which is analogous to that of an artificial elemental.

We are now in a position to understand the psychology of the untrained psychic; a part of his personality is dissociated for the purposes of his psychism. But whereas in the lunatic it is a part of the lower self which thus becomes separated, because it is felt to be too base for admittance to the fabric of coordinations which makes up the soul, in the case of the psychic it is a part of the higher self which thus becomes disconnected, because the rest of the personality is not sufficiently evolved to admit of its integration.

Although the cause is different, the result may end by being the same, for when once dissociation of personality is permitted to take place there is no saying how far it may continue. The little rift can become a deep fissure in a surprisingly short time.

The trained occultist is well aware of the power of the dissociated personality to obtain special psychic results, and he employs this faculty at his discretion. He knows that if he desires to function with a power of the soul which is not yet developed to an equal degree with the five physical senses he must close down those senses in order that the faint vibrations registered by the higher centres may become audible to consciousness instead of being swamped by the louder vibrations of a lower octave. He also knows that if he wants to hear the vibrations of the mental plane, he must close down the emotional reactions of the astral plane. He has a regular system of inducing those successive closings down, and it is known as "rising on the planes," and is produced by a concentration on the chosen plane of such a degree of intensity that all else is automatically excluded from consciousness. In this way he does not cause a faculty to split off and function independently, but inhibits all planes below the one on which he elects to operate, and the chosen faculty then functions in full correlation with the ego. A little thought will reveal the fundamental difference between this method and that of the naive psychic who allows a dissociation of personality to take place through repeated "projections" of mental images.

The trained occultist moreover, is exceedingly careful not to swim out farther than he can be sure of swimming back, for he knows that if the silver cord be loosed, the golden bowl of the integrity of the personality will be broken. He employs a regular system of connected ideas to carry consciousness up the planes by means of an association chain, and he comes down the planes by reversing the order of the images in his contemplation. He thus translates the symbolism accurately down the planes, and so the chain of associated ideas is not broken, and memory is brought through.

The highest development of occult work occurs when the objective consciousness of the different planes can be synthesised into a single chord as we synthesise the sensory consciousness of the physical plane when we see, hear, smell, and feel an object simultaneously, and out of this combination of impressions gain a far richer idea of the nature of that object than we could from any one of them taken singly.

For a full understanding of any form of existence, more than one plane of consciousness is necessary. The combined consciousness of the planes is to the psychic what binocular vision is to the ordinary mortal. For each added faculty of consciousness there is an added dimension of existence.

It is only the supreme adept, however, who is thus able to co-ordinate consciousness simultaneously; most occultists rely on the method already described of inhibiting the unwanted faculties until the desired one is laid bare and freed for function.

The weakness of the uninitiated psychic lies in the fact that he misunderstands his own modus operandi. Projection and dissociation, as already described, undermine the integrity of his mind. Moreover, by the method he uses he can only touch the fringe of the Unseen. Unlike the occultist, he cannot rise on the stepping stones of the symbols. He stops short at the first symbol that is evoked in consciousness, and that symbol may have little power of rendering the philosophical subtleties of the higher planes of mind.

Psychism is always limited by the contents of the psychic's subconscious mind. The spirit control is like an artist working in mosaic, he has to put his picture together out of little blocks of coloured marble and is limited by their characteristics. We therefore find that the psychic of limited intellectual content relies chiefly on picture consciousness for his symbols, whereas the more educated psychic brings through actual teaching in verbal form, the study for his subconscious content has been enriched by the study of the spoken and written word. It is not very common, however, to find psychics among highly educated people; when the mind is enriched by study it is also apt to be stereotyped, for the ideas received from its studies do not enter it as isolated units, but as parts of systems from which they cannot be detached. Therefore it is not possible for the spirit designer to rearrange the mosaic of his ideas to represent some new design. He cannot take a symbol from psychology and a symbol from dynamics and a symbol from religion and recombine them into a new concept to be represented to the mind. The integrated systems of the educated intellect resist this process. But where there can be found an educated mind with a wide range of intellectual content, wherein it is possible to close down the directive intelligence and permit the spirit entity to manipulate the images available in the subconscious memory, then is a high degree of mediumship possible.

Astral Psychism

The rending of the veil of the Temple has undoubtedly brought about some of the results that were dreaded by the upholders of occult secrecy. A little learning is as dangerous a thing in occultism as in any other line of study that gives practical results. It is not easy for the neophyte to assess the extent of his own knowledge. Particularly is this difficult in occultism, where but a partial revelation has been made. Moreover, the subject matter of esoteric science differs so completely from that which brain consciousness is accustomed to handle that a prolonged training is necessary to enable the mind to deal with it without distorting it, just as preparation is necessary for the comprehension of advanced mathematics or classical music.

Confusion is made worse confounded in esoteric studies by the fact that many of those who set up as teachers are not themselves initiates of any Tradition; they are "self-made men" with all the faulty technique and imperfect apprehensions which the self-taught are liable to acquire. More harm has been done to the cause of esoteric truth by the naive and superstitious concepts of it that have been spread abroad and popularised of recent years than by all the persecutions of the past, which, though they destroyed, did not pervert.

Judging by the questions heard at lectures, more confusion and misapprehension concerning the nature of the astral plane exist than concerning any other of the many debatable tenets of esoteric science. So many people regard the astral plane as an etherealised reproduction of the physical plane. They believe that their efforts at occult training will be rewarded by a glimpse of its denizens and visits to its palaces. This belief is inculcated and upheld by many writers who have large followings in esoteric circles and their romantic and spectacular teachings attract an uncritical public, which is always avid for romance. The serious thinker is estranged by such ideas, for he knows their intrinsic unsoundness, and so we see the occult field largely occupied by the credulous and the charlatan, and the scholar is conspicuous by his rarity.

Although several schools of esoteric thought derive their inspiration from the East, they seem to forget that Eastern philosophy has ever spoken of the astral plane as the realm of Maya, illusion, and regards its visions as among the chief fetters which the soul must break in order to win to freedom. Again, the astral plane is also known as the plane of Desire, and desire is always referred to as the bondage of the soul. When the immemorial occult tradition of the East adds its testimony to that of the West, surely it is time for the purveyors of spurious psychism to reconsider their doctrine.

To encourage any student in the development of astral psychism, which is recognisable by the pictorial or visual nature of its representations as distinguished from the intuitional realisations of the higher psychism, is to send that student down a blind alley. No true spiritual realisation is possible for him until he has retraced his steps. The habit of picture vision, once acquired, is not easy to break, and its practice tends more and more to bring about the dissociation of consciousness, which is the basis of nervous instability.

The study of the astral plane does not resemble the work of an exploring expedition, wherein the geographer draws his maps and the zoologist collects his specimens. We must try and disillusion our minds of the idea that the astral plane is a fantastic replica of the physical plane - "such stuff as dreams are made of." Actually, the study of the astral plane is a study in consciousness, and is pursued by the methods of psychology, not geography. It concerns the study of the emotional consciousness and the visualising power of the memory and imagination. The emotions and desires are the driving forces of the astral plane, and the visual imagination builds up the forms that embody them.

If we realise clearly that the forms seen by psychic vision on the astral plane are, without exception, thought-forms constructed by the visual imagination; are, in fact, "the creations of the created," we have the clue to the nature of Maya, illusion.

The difference between the initiate and the self-taught occultist lies in the fact that the former is fully alive to this all-important point, and the latter believes the forms seen with astral vision to be the actual objects which they represent. The Initiate, therefore, can manipulate at will the forms of the astral plane, for what the imagination has made, the imagination can influence. Secure in this knowledge, his attitude towards the astral form of existence enables him to manipulate it; he is its master, not its victim. The uninitiated psychic, functioning in astral consciousness, is entirely controlled by astral conditions; its hells fill him with horror and its heavens with delight. He looks to its denizens for teaching and guidance and receives from them the reflection of his own desires and fears. Whatever we expect on the astral plane, that we see.

The astral plane is the plane of emotion, and emotion is the only reality thereon existing. If you want to understand and master the astral plane, look upon it simply as emotional experience; control the spontaneous emotional reactions of your own nature; learn to generate emotion at will from the contemplation of an idea, and the astral image-forms will fall into line at your command, for it is emotion that causes them to assume their forms, and if emotion can be controlled, the manifestation in astral form can be determined, subject, of course, to the natural laws of the astral plane, which are really its inherent nature, and not arbitrary enactments.

The difficulty of astral control in actual practice lies in the fact that the emotions are deep-rooted in the natural instincts of self-preservation and reproduction, and that the herd-mind of the race holds many highly organised emotional complexes. Hence, the significance of Our Lord's words that he who would find his life must lose it. Only when we are indifferent to the lure of the instincts can we manipulate the driving-forces which are generated by the instincts. It is to induce this power of emotional control that the disciplinary and ascetic practices of the occultist are undertaken.

There are two types of emotion, that which is the reaction to a sensation, or a remembered or anticipated sensation, and that which is the reaction to an idea. The former is derived from without, and the latter originates within. The aim of the adept and the yogi is to acquire the power to inhibit the reaction to external impressions and thus to reverse the flow of influence between himself and his environment; as soon as he ceases to react emotionally to his environment he becomes able to influence it by means of his thoughts. As long as he reacts emotionally, his attitude towards the not-self is negative; receptive; reverse the polarity, let him cease to react, and he becomes positive to a negative environment, which must accept its stimuli from him. Every word that he speaks then becomes a Word of Power. Every thought he formulates is potent. Let him teach himself such thought-control that he will not react to emotion; let him look for the mental cause behind all phenomena so constantly that the habit of mind engendered becomes second nature to him, thus breaking the habits of thought built up by sensory experience, and he will become the master of the astral, for he will be able to distinguish between the actuality and the representation.

The Psychology of Clairvoyance

When a psychic tells us that he "sees" a presence, to us invisible, how are we to understand that statement? The veridical nature of many of these visions prevents us from disposing of them summarily. Whatever alloy of fraud and phantasy there may be, a residuum of genuine metal will undoubtedly remain after the smelting. To seek to understand the process where by a result is achieved does not necessarily mean that the result is explained away. A thing is explained away only when the whole of its being and doing can be explained in terms of something else, and nothing remains which is peculiar to itself. If a ghost can be resolved into a turnip, a sheet, and a broomstick, it has been explained away, but if we have to introduce the word ectoplasm, it has not. We must then begin the study of ectoplasm, which is a thing peculiar to supernormal phenomena.

We must distinguish, first of all, between etheric and astral psychism. There is a subtle form of matter, today being extensively investigated by physicists, which has long been known to occultists, and which forms the basis of much super-normal phenomena. Occultists refer to it as the Etheric sub-planes of the physical plane, recognising various sub-classes into which it can be divided, and spiritualists call it ectoplasm. The emanations of this form of existence are being extensively studied by the physicist, who bids fair to meet the occultist on his own ground before very long. Instruments have been designed which will register these emanations, and many of the statements of psychics regarding their perceptions have been verified. It appears, therefore, that the type of psychism which is able to see the emanations radiating from living bodies depends upon an increase in the sensitiveness of the eye, and not upon any super-normal faculty of the mind. These emanations are of a wavelength, which exceeds the normal reception-power of the eye, and therefore pass unnoticed by it, just as many ears cannot hear the high shrill note of a bat's squeak. Increase the range of perception, and the hitherto unperceived vibrations are picked up.

Though etheric sight can be both explained and confirmed by modern physics, psychic vision remains in a different category. For although the photographic plate will confirm etheric sight, the complex vision pictures seem individual to the seer, and although there may be sufficient agreement to show that two seers may both be trying to render the same experience, there is never, so far as my own investigations extend, at any rate, precise agreement in all details, as there would be if two photographers took a photograph of the same object. How are we to explain both the agreement and the disagreement?

Let us first of all try to understand something of the psychology of normal vision, and so how the mind works in relation to the impressions that come to it through the eye.

Rays of light are reflected from an object on to the eye and focus through the lens upon the retina. The cells of the retina, which are sensitive to light, react to it, and the reaction is carried as an electrical impulse, along the optic nerve to a certain set of cells in the brain. There it is perceived as a sensation of a particular type, just as the sensations carried by the auditory nerve to the ear are perceived as sound, and sensations from the nerves of the surface of the body are perceived as heat, cold, and touch.

Curious as it may seem to those untrained in science, sensation exists solely in the brain. The burnt finger feels nothing in itself. Cut off its communication with the brain by severing the nerve fibres that serves it, and it could be charred to a cinder without sensation. Operations on the lower parts of the body are often performed under an anaesthetic injected into the lower part of the spinal cord.

The patient is fully conscious of all impressions reaching the nerves which enter the spinal cord above that point, but the lower parts of his body are without sensation or power of movement, and he can watch his own flesh being cut as impersonally as if it belonged to some one else.

A general anaesthetic, such as chloroform, acts on the brain-centres, however, and therefore all consciousness and power of movement is cut off, but those nerve impulses which do not connect with the brain, but serve the involuntary muscles of heart, lungs, and intestines, go on as usual.

From these considerations we see that the Ego is dependent for its impressions of the physical plane, and for its activities thereon, on the machinery of the brain and nervous system, and that if any part of this very complex and beautifully contrived machine be thrown out of gear, consciousness is cut off from that aspect of the physical plane. It is also important to note that each type of nerve fibre is adapted to carry, and each centre in the brain is adapted to receive, a certain type and range of stimuli only. There is no accommodation between the nerves to carry each other's messages.

Sound, however loud, will not make a blind man see. Light, however bright, will not make a deaf man hear. A stimulus is only perceived when it falls upon the appropriate sense organ. In the absence of that organ, that particular stimulus does not exist so far as that person is concerned.

A deaf man will be oblivious of the sound which throws a normal man into a paroxysm of fear. A musician with cultivated aesthetic gifts will be exalted by sounds which make no particular impression on the uneducated. A psychic will be uplifted or distressed by that of which the man of average nervous sensibility is blissfully unaware. Nevertheless, the stimuli, whether observed or not, are about all three all the time. Increase the sensitivity of the perception and the stimuli will be perceived.

Finally, in this respect, it is to be noted that any stimulus applied to a nerve-fibre will produce the specific sensation associated with the action of the stimulus. For instance, an electric shock to the eye produces a sensation of blinding light; so, it is recorded, does the severance of the optic nerve by the surgeon's knife. The action of any corrosive chemical on the skin produces a sensation of burning although no heat is present. A lunatic, unable to correlate his ideas correctly, declared that the fires of hell were within his chest when suffering from pneumonia. These incidents throw much light on the psychic's vision, as will be seen later.

The stimulus received from the not-self produces a series of reactions which culminate in a final reaction in a certain area in the brain. That reaction we call sensation and sensation we will define for our purposes as the reaction of the ego to changes in its physical vehicle. The manner in which the translation of impulse from the physical to the mental takes place has never been explained by natural science, though it is not disputed that such a translation does take place. Esoteric science, however, has a formula by means of which it explains the translation of force between the planes of existence. That formula would no doubt permit of far greater elaboration then the present writer is able to give it, but it will at least enable us to do what the mathematician does in handling an unknown quantity or proportion, and represent it by a symbol which enables the transition from one aspect to another of the calculation to be made accurately and conveniently; if the symbol gives rise to no discrepancy, we may reasonably conclude that it is a true representation of that which it represents, and that if x or y were translated into figures, they would yield the truth.

A brief explanation of the esoteric doctrine of translation between the planes must here be given, in order that the reader may be able to follow the line of the argument.

It is held by esoteric science, and in this it is in agreement with natural science, that all existence is but one or another form of force. Each type of force has its wavelength, or vibration-ratio. Different ranges of vibration-ratio give different types of existence. These different types of wavelength are perceived by sense-organs that correspond to them, and these sense organs give rise to different types of consciousness in the sentient ego. The vibration of wavelengths of a certain register are picked up only by the tactile nerves; those of another register by the olfactory nerves; those of yet another cease to be on the physical sub-planes of the material plane, but are of a rate of vibration which belongs to the etheric scale, and are picked up by the eye, which is attuned to that scale.

This brings us to the consideration of the not uncommon instance of people who invariably associate certain colours with certain musical notes; from this let us next pass on to the almost universal association of certain emotions with certain chords and rhythms. The esotericists would explain these phenomena by saying that there was a certain ratio-relationship between them. For instance, were the vibration-rate of the musical note in question, for the sake of argument, x to the second, the rate of vibration of the colour which corresponded to it would be x_2 to the second, and of the emotion which also corresponded to it, x_3 to the second.

Working on this formula, the esotericist assigns a vibration rate to all forms of existence. Each plane is covered by a certain section of the vibration scale. In order to transpose an object from one form of existence to another, its vibration must be multiplied if ascending the planes, and divided if descending them, but always the exact ratio must be maintained. The method by which this is accomplished cannot be entered upon at the moment, for it is outside the scope of our argument, though an appreciation of its rationale is essential to the argument. Let it be realised, however, that there is a ratio-relationship between form, number, sound, colour, emotion, and idea. It is this ratio which forms the basis of the presentations of psychic vision.

The Real Nature of Vision

It is a fundamental maxim in psychology that nothing can enter consciousness save through the gates of the senses. At first sight the mystic is inclined to dispute this statement, but a moment's thought will reveal to him its truth, and he will join issue with the materialist, not upon the maxim itself, but upon the number and nature of the avenues of approach to the ego.

In these pages we are not attempting to prove the actuality of psychism to the sceptic; rather are we "preaching to the converted" and trying to help them to arrive at a better understanding of the true nature of the phenomena of clairvoyance which we have agreed to accept as proven.

Our surest guide in such a research is to consider what has already been arrived at concerning the psychology of vision in relation to the physical plane, and thence to extend our researches by analogy to the subtler planes.

Let us reduce our problem to its simplest form, and watch a newborn child learning to use its eyes. At first he can but distinguish between light and darkness; soon he begins to perceive form and colour and to associate them with pleasure and pain. But he cannot yet judge distance by perspective, and will stretch out his hands to grasp any object that attracts him, however far away. He is obviously and rapidly learning by experience. He perceives an object, and remembers it, so that when he sees it again, he recognises it. He also recognises as familiar anything which closely resembles it. What have these facts to teach us concerning the psychology of vision?

On the assumption of our previous hypotheses concerning translation between the planes, we should say that the composite vibration-ratio of the object perceived, simplified as it probably is by the inexperienced eye, is translated into its equivalent ratio on a higher octave, and thus a mental form is created. This mental picture forms part of the furnishing of the consciousness of the personality, which, like an empty house built of the innate qualities brought through from previous incarnations, awaits the fittings which shall render it a well-equipped dwelling for the Ego.

Each mental picture added to the collection forms the basis for the apprehension and classification of each succeeding impression.

A new object is recognised as resembling in certain particulars that which was previously known and differing from it in certain others. The mental classification takes place; and until it takes place we cannot be said to "know" a thing but only to perceive it. By means of the recognition of resemblance and difference, perception becomes conception, and an image takes its place in the mind.

A stock of images is rapidly built up in this way. The child, with the passage of time, becomes able to tell a horse from a dog, and also to classify together a white horse and a white dog, as distinguished from a black horse and a black dog.

The eye soon becomes accustomed to work by means of a kind of shorthand; it sees some salient feature with which it is familiar, and concludes that the other familiar features which it is accustomed to associate with it are also present, and the familiar mental image rises in consciousness in all its completeness; even though distance or a dim light has prevented it from being actually seen in detail by the eye, memory and imagination supply what is lacking.

It is very important for the clear understanding of the psychology of vision that we should understand that we actually "perceive" but a very small proportion of what we visualise; we do not build a fresh mental image carefully and elaborately each time a ray of light falls on the retina; mind co-operates with brain, and the mental pictures spring up full-grown, like Minerva from the head of Jove. Experimental psychology soon demonstrates to us how much of our so-called "seeing" is really a stimulation of memory, and we are not looking at the thing before us, but at the mental picture it has caused to rise in our minds. How many people have been surprised to perceive one day in a familiar object some detail that must have been there all the time, but which they had never seen before? People vary very much in this respect; the keen, alert-minded person actually sees much more of what is before him than does the dreamy one; the latter sees what he expects and misses altogether what he does not expect. The former depends more on his senses, the latter on his memories.

We are now in a position to return once again to the consideration of the subject of our study, the nature of psychic vision, having informed ourselves concerning the nature of vision in general.

Let us take it as proven that there are individuals who can perceive stimuli that the average person cannot, just as the sensitive plate of the camera can perceive rays beyond the normal spectrum, which the human eye is unable to see. The stimuli perceived by these rare persons are of such a different octave to those which the physical senses pick up, that we feel justified in assigning them to another plane of existence. We are therefore equally justified in assuming that the mechanism of their reception may justly be classed as another sense organ.

Now, how does this sense organ operate? By observation of psychics we find that the principles of its operation are precisely analogous to those which govern the operations of the five physical senses with which we are already familiar. We may assume, then, that the stimuli are received by a sense organ adapted to their perception, and translated into terms of consciousness by the method of ratio-analogy we have already studied.

Are these impressions transmitted to the brain? Is there a centre in the cortex which is adapted to receive psychic stimuli, just as there are centres specialised for the reception of auditory and visual stimuli? This question opens up an enormous field of research and speculation; all that can be done in these pages is briefly to state my hypothesis in order to enable the argument to be pursued.

I am of the opinion that the brain is the organ of sensory perception and motor co-ordination, and is therefore the organ of contact with the physical plane, but it is to the Ego that we must look as the seat of consciousness. When the Ego is withdrawn, as in certain forms of insanity, physical impressions, even such as the pain of acute appendicitis, may be unperceived.

We may then conceive of each state of consciousness (subtle body) having its own mode of reacting to external stimuli (sense organs and nervous system) and its own system of ratio-symbols for translating these impressions into egoic consciousness (brain). We can see, then, the Ego itself, the sole centre of consciousness, gathering up the impressions coming in through each of these sets of sense organs and brains, each reacting to its own type of stimuli, just as the physical brain gathers up and co-ordinates the impressions received from the different sense organs of the physical body.

In order to understand the nature of the substance of a plane, we must apply to it the same methods as physical science has applied to research into the fundamental nature of the substance of the physical plane. We know that the physical senses, unaided by instruments of precision, are not able to render more than a very superficial account of the physical plane, and that when the methods of exact science are applied to that plane, we find that the real nature of matter is very different from the appearance it presents to the untrained observer. So it is with the subtler planes. The actual nature of the substance and entities of these planes is not perceived by the untrained psychic any more than the real nature of the atom is discerned by the eye of the average man.

The astral plane undoubtedly presents to the consciousness of the psychic the *appearances* which have been so often described, but the occult scientist knows that these appearances are in the eye of the beholder alone, and do not represent actualities, save symbolically.

Consciousness of the Planes

It is agreed by physicists that all that actually exists on the physical plane is force; matter in its different forms is simply the appearance which force, in its different aspects, presents to the senses. The same is equally true of the subtler planes of existence. They are simply different types of force with their various sub-divisions, and the impression we get of them is the affect they produce on our consciousness.

The type of existence of each plane is indicated by the name given to it. On the mental plane, thought is the basic substance; on the astral plane, emotion is the basic substance, or, in other words, all thought exists on the mental plane, and nothing else exists there; and all emotion exists on the astral plane, and nothing else exists there.

We use the word "plane" for these different aspects of existence because it is the term that has been established by usage, but it is in many ways an unfortunate term and leads to misapprehension because it teaches us to think of the different types of existence as lying one above the other like the layers of the atmosphere, whereas the different "planes" are really but different modes of manifestation of force. Each "keeps itself to itself" in that it only acts and reacts among its own type of existence, and is oblivious of all other types save when translations are made up and down the planes by the modes we have described. Consciousness, however, even the most rudimentary consciousness, synthesises the modes of existence rendered available for it by its composite nature and reacts to them as an integration, not as units. If, however, consciousness desires to act upon its environment, it cannot deal with it as integration, but must separate it into units. Hence the custom of the occultist who speaks of the "planes" of the universe, and teaches his consciousness to think of them as separate worlds. As we think of things on the inner planes, so they are, and if he thinks of them as separate, he disentangles his apprehension of them and is able to contact them separately. This was the discipline of the Lesser Mysteries, which taught its initiates to conceive of the planes separately in order that they might be able to deal with individual factors. It is this doctrine which has been given out to the world by partially initiated students. The higher degrees of the Mysteries, however, gave the key of a philosophical concept. It is this key which is lacking to the naive occultists who accept the plane of illusion at its face value.

Very large proportions of the people who are now studying occultism are quite incapable of grasping this philosophic concept. They get as far as a realisation of the existence of worlds which their eyes cannot see, and they immediately conceive of these worlds as being exactly like our own if they could see them. They do not realise that these worlds are not kept separate from our familiar earth by the occupation of a difference position in space, but are separated from it by being of an entirely different mode of existence, and that if we chose to speak of them in terms of position in space, which, strictly speaking, we should not do, for it is misleading, we should be obliged to say that the different forms of existence were not only interpenetrating, but occupied exactly the same spot without necessarily affecting each other in the very slightest, and that they are not in the least mutually exclusive. This can only take place in the crucible of consciousness, and it takes place normally wherever there is life. It is the projection of consciousness into the not-self which is one of the processes of practical occultism.

The initiate is distinguished from the uninitiated occultist by the fact that he sees through the symbol to the reality it represents. The Hindu mystic resents the allegation of the missionary that he worships an idol. He declares that he does not, but seeks, by focusing his mind on a symbol, to contact the potency which that symbol represents, and thereby to bring its influence into his life. It is not, he declares, the fault of his faith that the limitations of the uneducated cause them to present a naive concept of the Hindu philosophy to the questioning missionary; no Hindu pundit would take their statements seriously. So it is with occultism. The word "idol" comes from the Greek *eidolon* which means an image; the initiate knows that the image perceived by the *imag - ination* of the psychic is on a par with the image worshipped by the Hindu. Both images are made by the worshipper to provide a focusing point for the contact of a force. To look upon the image as the reality is to be an idolater, whether you are a savage or an occultist.

The Dawn of the Higher Consciousness

We talk glibly of spirit and the spiritual, but can we give an account of it which is intelligible to others, even if we ourselves know what we mean by these words, which is very often not the case? Even the Oxford English Dictionary cannot do better than define it by negatives as that which is immaterial. When spirit is equated with God, we are not much better off, as God is defined again in negatives as a superhuman being. We are working in a circle, and "come out by the same door wherein we went."

I propose to define spirit as synonymous with life and life as synonymous with spirit. Spirit is the pure essence of life, and life as it is known to us is spirit expressed through the machinery of a form; spirit, then, is unembodied life, and life is unembodied spirit. We have now something tangible on which to work, for we have but to examine the characteristics of upbuilding life, to be able to deduce something of the nature of God, of spirit, and to go on from height to height as our powers of intuitive deduction shall enable us; and on the other hand, we have but to examine the phenomena of down-breaking life to understand something of the functions of Death and the Devil. We shall then see that Life and Spirit and Death and Devil are but complementary processes of the one cyclic rhythm. Nevertheless, we are not duellists, contemplating an unresolved antagonism, but see both these pairs of opposites as modes of existence, which differ, not in essence, but in direction, one is on the outgoing and the other on the returning arc of the circle.

Our surface-consciousness is habituated to the task of dealing with impressions received from the physical senses; it is only in comparatively rare souls that it is able to synthesise the impressions coming in dimly and faintly from the subtler senses hidden in the deeps of consciousness. Nevertheless it is possible to habituate it to these impressions by resolutely and persistently attending to them and by exercising our minds on all that is akin to their nature which other minds have translated into terms of brain-consciousness for us. A mind thus exercised and practised soon builds up a stock of images which corresponds to the impressions received through the subtler sense, and learns to perceive and interpret them with facility.

Such attaining must have a beginning. We have to take the mind from where it is at present, immersed in impressions derived from the sensations of matter, and teach it to perceive and focus impressions derived from much subtler forms of existence. Normally, it is only adapted to register the workings of the machinery of life. We have got to teach it to perceive life itself if we are to arrive at spiritual consciousness.

In order to achieve this consciousness we must train the mind to think of life apart from physical form and to realise that a consciousness, or organised system of reactions and memories, persists after bodily death. This lesson spiritualism has taught to the world, and offers evidence in proof of it for individual consideration by those who desire to transcend the limits of materialism. Next we may call upon the mind to consider, and if possible to experiment with, the phenomena of telepathy; when we can ask it to go on to the study of the power of the mind over the body, as exemplified by auto-suggestion, and to experiment with this too. Thus the mind is gradually weaned from its submergence in matter and its complete dependence upon the five physical senses. "As the mind thinks, so is it." If it believes itself to be limited to the perceptions of the five physical senses, so it will be; but if it conceives the possibility of the extension of perception to include states of existence, not cognised by those senses, consciousness will be extended to include them. The first step in the opening of the psychic faculties is the realisation that we have them.

But psychism is not of the kingdom of the spirit, it still concerns the things of the mind. Nevertheless the man who has realised the possibility of another mode of consciousness than that of matter will be the more ready to realise the existence of another mode of consciousness than that of mind. For mind is but another, though more subtle, vehicle of life, and not life itself. Life, as the Oxford Dictionary truly recognises in its definition, is distinct from form. That which we distinguish as forms is essentially not life.

How, then, are we to perceive life itself? In the same way that we distinguish the modes of existence on the other planes - by the reaction which the corresponding aspect of our own composite nature makes to it. We perceive material things by the reactions of our physical vehicle, and we perceive spiritual things by the reactions of our spiritual nature, which responds to their stimulus by manifesting the qualities of the essence it contacts. As we touch Love, so are we loving; as we touch Life, so are we living.

Habituated, as we are to mind consciousness, we cannot conceive of any other form of awareness. For us, nothing is apprehended unless it is focused by the mind. But there are forms of consciousness which are both inferior and superior to mind consciousness. Emotional consciousness may consist of emotional reactions with no tincture of thought; it may be stimulated by the emotion of another with no word spoken, no sign exchanged. Normally, in intellectually developed people, such emotional reactions, belonging to a lower grade of evolution, are translated into terms of mind consciousness because the ego focuses on the plane of the concrete mind, but in times of stress they may sometimes be perceived in their primitive form, and are very instructive.

Equally with the impressions derived from the world of spirit; we are so accustomed to focus in the concrete mind that we cannot habituate ourselves to the idea of a form of apprehension which is not mental. Therefore the things of the spirit are a closed book to us; it requires a long training to enable us to raise consciousness to the spiritual plane and to "know even as we are known" and we have at first to be content to see "as in a glass, darkly." This glass is the subconscious mind, the magic mirror of the occultists. In it rise the thought-forms stimulated by the impressions received through the subtler senses. If we are receiving impressions from the plane of spirit, it may be that vision will result as we gaze into the magic mirror of our own subconscious mind. But no vision which is expressed in terms of sensory images can be a direct perception of the plane of spirit; it can only be a symbolic rendering, for there are no forms in spirit.

If we are content to look into the magic mirror, we shall never rise into the higher consciousness. If we cultivate the magic mirror, we may sink into a lower form of consciousness which involves dissociation of the higher faculties. Nevertheless, the magic mirror may be our first link with supernal realities, the means by which a realisation of non-physical forms of existence is borne in upon us.

Once we have a realisation of such a reality (and this realisation can only be brought about by definite experience, however vague and fleeting, it can never result from intellectual conviction,) we have won a foothold in the Unseen, and we can begin to explore in all directions; but without such a foothold, we have no means of making a start.

Nevertheless, the tendency of the mind to bring all things to a focus in concrete consciousness must be sternly resisted - until the habit is broken - if we are to win an apprehension of spiritual realities. Although a better understanding of emotional states is gained if we intellectualise them and translate them into terms of ideas, the apprehension of spiritual states is prevented when we try so to intellectualise them, for we are debasing them in the attempt. Emotion is raised when it is translated into terms of mind, but spiritual consciousness is lowered, and its true significance clouded.

If we want to develop spiritual consciousness, as distinguished from mental and astral consciousness, we must remember that ideas and sensory images play no part in it. Its nearest equivalent is in feeling, and it is in states of exalted feeling directed towards non-mundane objects that we find our best realisation of spiritual consciousness.

The esotericist distinguishes two planes of spirit, and such a distinction makes the concept much more apprehensible. He recognises the plane of pure Spirit, which is ineffable and formless, where "All are one and One is all" and distinguishes from this the plane of Concrete Spirit, which consists of the qualities which Spirit manifests. This distinction between Spirit and its qualities is of great practical importance to the seeker after mystic consciousness, for although it is impossible for finite consciousness, the consciousness of the personality built up through the experiences of the senses, to apprehend pure Spirit, it is within its power, when trained, to comprehend spiritual qualities, or, in the language of esoteric science, to rise to the Sixth Plane, or Plane of Concrete Spirit. These it comprehends in proportion as it possesses them; hence the significance of the old saying, "Lead the life and you will understand the doctrine." For a consciousness habituated to the Plane of Concrete Spirit, that is to say, to the expression of the spiritual qualities in a Christ-like life, there is much evidence available that it is possible to rise to the Plane of Pure Spirit and "see God face to face."

COMMENTARY

Dion Fortune became interested in psychology when coming to terms with the symptoms of a nervous breakdown induced at a residential college by a bullying employer with a knowledge of what would now be called brain washing techniques. Having got through this as best she might, and it would seem successfully, she applied herself seriously to the study of psychoanalysis. At this time, in the years immediately before the First World War, Freud's theories of the subconscious were making a considerable impact upon society.

With the intention of building up a practice as a lay analyst she attended classes at the University of London and undertook clinical work under the auspices of the London (Royal Free Hospital) School of Medicine for Women. She seems to have been quite successful in this endeavour, to the extent of being asked to give public lectures, some of which were collected and published as "The Machinery of the Mind" in 1922 under her maiden name of Violet M.Firth. A distinguished scientist, A.G.Tansley, provided a foreword.

However, she found in that in some of her case work certain phenomena could not be explained by accepted psychological theories alone. This led her to the study of occultism, which she pursued in as thorough and practical a manner as she had psychology, leading eventually to her forming an experimental group at Glastonbury which became, in time, the Society of the Inner Light.

During her early years at Glastonbury in 1921/2 she met Frederick Bligh Bond and the records show that they performed some psychical work together with herself acting as medium. Bond had for some years been concerned with archaeological excavation work at Glastonbury Abbey where he had caused considerable misgivings amongst the ecclesiastical authorities for his use of psychic methods. Most of this had taken place however before his meeting with Dion Fortune however, and he was at this time in the last stages of his association with Glastonbury Abbey.

Bligh Bond was also connected with the College of Psychic Science (now the College of Psychic Studies) and edited their journal "Psychic Science". It was in his capacity as editor of an allied publication, "Quarterly Transactions of the B.P.S." that he published a long article by Dion Fortune in the issue for July 1922. Written under the name in which she was known in psychological circles, Violet M. Firth, it was entitled "Psychology and Occultism". Here she makes a spirited defence against the materialist trend of "behaviourism" that was beginning to take over orthodox thinking in psychology, and seeks to draw more attention to the esoteric side of consciousness.

PSYCHOLOGY AND OCCULTISM
by Violet M. Firth

Before a matter can be discussed it is necessary that the terms employed should be defined, and especially is this necessary when such debatable subjects as psychology and occultism are being considered.

Psychology is the youngest of the sciences to assume a scientific form; its development was slow and tentative until the publication of Freud's book upon the interpretation of dreams and his system of psycho-analysis gave us an instrument of precision for the investigation of the human mind. In its early days it was considered, as the name implies, the science which investigated the soul. In Professor McDougal's definition, however, which has had much currency of recent years this bold undertaking has been modified, and psychology declared to be the study of behaviour.

To my mind this definition is too narrow, unless one includes all forms of mental activity from intuition to phantasy-making under the heading of behaviour, and I propose, for the purposes of this essay to use the term psychology to connote the study of mental phenomena from the standpoint of inductive science.

By the world Occultism I indicate that body of doctrine, method and data which has come down to us by the tradition of the initiates, and I also include under this heading the phenomena which this tradition has always regarded as its especial territory, but which is now being investigated by spiritualists and psychic research workers.

No one who has attempted the practical exploration of these two subjects can fail to note the extent to which they overlap. Psychology approaches the human mind by the empirical method, and occultism makes use of it according to certain theories handed down by tradition.

It is my belief that each of these fellow-workers in the same field can be of enormous assistance to the other if they will lay aside their mutual pride and suspicion and consent to co-operate. Psychology regards the occult manifestations as the fraud of charlatans and delusion of hysterics, and occultism resents this attitude towards its phenomena by those who, in the great majority of cases, have never troubled to investigate that which they condemn, and despises psychology for its limitation of outlook.

It cannot be held that the psychologist is entirely blame-worthy in this respect. It must be remembered that of the phenomena presented for his inspection, a large part will not bear the test of scientific investigation; much of the most important of psychic investigation is practised under conditions which do not permit of scientific exactness, and as Bergson pointed out in his presidential address to the S.P.R., the method of psychic research has to be historical rather than scientific. It must also be remembered that the medium, upon whom the psychic research-worker is dependent for most of his phenomena, is a person of peculiar mental constitution, and is exceedingly subject to mental and nervous trouble, so that when the psychologist sees unmistakable signs of nervous instability in the person who exhibits the phenomena, he is tempted to attribute the whole of the manifestations to this cause, and discredit the entire affair. It never occurs to him to see what light the psychology of mediumship can throw upon the problem of mental disease.

Occultism, on the other hand, is apt to accept all its phenomena in an almost religious spirit, and it is considered almost sacrilegious to throw doubt upon the messages that come through the trance medium or automatic writer. It resents the cold water thrown by scientific methods, which brings it down to earth just as it is scaling the heights of heaven. Yet it cannot be denied that mediums are hysterical and sitters suggestible.

It is my contention that psychology can be of great service to occult investigation by counterchecking its results, and that the occult theories can give psychology much light upon the organisation of the mind.

For the purposes of a rough classification I have divided the occult phenomena into the following five divisions:-

I The poltergeist type. Table turning, spirit rapping, levitation, the moving of objects, and materialisation mediumship.
II Phenomena of the transmission or translation type, such as automatic writing and trance speaking.
III Direct perception, without the intervention of any of the physical senses, such as telepathy, psychometry, and the reading of the "Akashic" records.
IV The action of individuals that do not possess a physical vehicle and of individuals that have the power of withdrawing from their physical vehicle.
V The theory of reincarnation or metempsychosis and the doctrine of Kharma or causation.

These are the phenomena of which occultism claims the existence and offers its own explanation in accordance with its traditional doctrines, whereas orthodox science sweeps the whole lot away as fraud and delusions and refuses to investigate them. The question of their verity I do not propose to enter upon here, the reader must refer to the many excellent books that exist upon the subject, and which set forth the carefully verified evidence in such abundance that I should think any unprejudiced mind must be convinced of the existence of certain supernormal phenomena, whether it accepts the occult explanation or not.

With regard to my own position in this matter, I may say that I have personally seen enough of such phenomena to convince me that they do occur, and that I largely accept the occult theories with regard to them. I also believe that these occult theories, robbed of their verbiage, can be translated into terms of psychology without any contradiction between the two schools of thought.

But it has been my experience that much of the phenomena presented to us as occult phenomena though not of a fraudulent nature, is purely subjective and can be best interpreted in terms of psychology.

It must not be forgotten, however, that the subjective phenomena are of extraordinary interest, and throw great light upon hitherto unsuspected capacities of the human mind.

Now to consider the different types of occult phenomena.

Class I is of extraordinary interest and importance, because, to my mind, it represents the point of contact between mind and matter. All these phenomena point to the existence of a substance which, while not material in the usual understanding of the term, is yet capable of acting upon dense matter, exerting pressure and sustaining weight. It is generally held, in spiritualistic circles, that this substance is used by discarnate entities to mould themselves bodies and so become visible to those who are still in the flesh. I do not wish to discredit this idea, because it is my belief that it can and does occur, but I wish to advance a subsidiary theory, which I believe throws additional light upon the matter, and explains certain difficulties which have arisen in this connection. It is my belief that this substance, either visible or invisible, which exudes from the medium and also very frequently from the sitters, belongs to what occultists call the etheric sub-division of the physical plane, and it is believed by them that this form of matter is capable of being moulded by mind and is used by them as the basis of certain of their phenomena. Those who are acquainted with the literature of the subject cannot fail to be struck by the fact that the undirected phenomena of the poltergeist and a certain type of séance when odds and ends fly about without physical cause, is of the same type as the purposive results recorded as being obtained by the adepts of the occult arts. These claim to obtain their results by operating mentally upon the etheric form of matter; supposing we take this theory as a working hypothesis, and see where it leads us.

The spirits of the dead, which are minds without bodies, would be able to use this medium as a means of influencing dense matter and so making themselves apparent to the physical senses, but the minds of incarnated spirits, the living would likewise affect it, and just as the discarnate mind can mould a representation of itself in this form of matter, so the living mind can form an image of its memory of the dead upon which it may be concentrating. And although we may get the actual spirit entity functioning through this form, we may also get nothing but a product of the subconscious mind of a sitter in the séance, a concept much more acceptable to many of us who believe that the great majority of the dead are in a subjective or sleeping condition after death, and that only the more developed type of individual is capable of active functioning upon other planes; that is to say, the man who is incapable of function on another plane during life will be equally incapable of functioning actively after death, and will not, therefore, make himself known through the séance medium; on the other hand, if he be capable of functioning on these planes of activity during life, then he would go over in full possession of his consciousness, and would be quite capable of manifesting through a suitable medium, or even directly upon the subconscious minds of those still in the flesh, though whether they were aware of it or not depends upon their capacity to get in touch with their own subconscious minds.

This theory would explain the peculiar instance of the photograph of Miss Scatcherd, who, at the moment of the exposure, thought of a lace coat which she wished she had with her, and the dim ghost of the lace coat occurred on the negative. It would also explain the phenomena of the newspaper headlines and pictures from an illustrated paper, which appeared in the materialisations of "Mdlle. Eva C.," and caused so much criticism. It is true that both these occurrences are incompatible with the theory that we are engaged with a form of matter, the etheric, which is capable of being influenced by mind, whether that mind is incarnate or discarnate being immaterial.

Likewise, this theory has a profound bearing upon the problem of disease. Occultists teach that these ethers are the vehicles of the life forces; if they are influenced by the mind, as we believe them to be, then we have the clue to the phenomena of mental healing and faith cures. What would cancer research yield if it studied the problem on the supposition of an etheric body? Supposing the diseases of metabolism were studied in relation to the hypothesis of the chemical ether which occultists teach to be the medium of the life processes of assimilation and elimination. I do not put these occult doctrines forward as established facts, I simply suggest that science should take them as working hypotheses and see whither they lead; it is a method which I have applied to my own study of psychology with most interesting results.

II. - Automatic writing and trance speaking. These two phenomena are regarded as being methods of communication with planes other than the material and with the beings that function upon those planes. It is the occult theory that the medium who submits to this method of manipulation either lifts right out of his body and permits other minds to act upon his material vehicle, throwing the vocal cords into vibration or he becomes so passive that his mind is acted upon by other entities and translates their messages. To these I will add a third hypothesis, that a second personality of the medium may come into function under certain conditions, and that this secondary personality may be of superior calibre to the normal personality because it has the subconscious memory storehouse to draw upon. When we recollect that every idea that has ever been in the mind is registered in the subconscious, as is proved by hypnosis and psychoanalysis, and if we also accept the theory that the fruits of the previous incarnation of the soul are also stored in a certain level of the subconscious, then we can see what riches the mind has access to if it can only get in contact with its own subconscious level, without any need to go beyond them.

In entering the trance condition one sees the medium become abstracted, and then, closing down the avenues of the five physical senses, enter a subjective state. In some mediums one can observe this condition very well, especially when it is the intention to get trance speech, the contact is maintained with the vocal organs. One hears scraps of undirected talk connected with the medium's own affairs, his subconscious wishes and anxieties; then, very often, one hears him contact the memories of previous incarnations, and thence pass out of his subjective condition and become objective upon another plane. It must be remembered, however, that there is more than one plane of superphysical manifestation, each of which is capable of being contacted by the appropriate state of consciousness, known as the seven hypnoidal levels. These levels correspond to the etheric plane, whereon we get the spirit-rapping phenomena; the lower astral, which is usually the level of extremely undesirable manifestations; the upper astral, the commonest level of mediumship, whereon are met discarnate entities that are neither strikingly bad nor good, and seldom of much intelligence; the lower mental, whereon the trained occultist usually begins to function and entities of a much higher intellectual type are contacted; this is the level of concrete thought, and most interesting and valuable information can be obtained by working subjectively upon this level; the upper mental, the level of abstract thought is sacred to a very high degree of intelligence, and is not often contacted save by a high order of occultist; no one can go to this plane voluntarily, he has to be taken there by the cooperation of some intelligence of that plane; the lower spiritual, the plane of the *Logoi,* exceedingly seldom contacted, and only for purposes of cosmic work; anyone who has had the privilege of contacting this plane will carry the mark of it to his grave.

It will be seen from this brief description that all trance work is not of equal value, it depends upon the level upon which the medium is working, and mediums usually have their special level; for instance, one will specialise upon the etheric plane and produce materialising phenomena, while another will use the lower mental and have access to an intellectual type of communication. I do not propose to enter upon the study of these hypnoidal states, and I have merely enumerated them in order to enable myself to point out their relationship to psychology, and show where the criticism of the psychological method can be of great value in determining the objectivity of phenomena; I do not say "the genuineness of phenomena," because phenomena can be perfectly genuine examples of subconscious conditions, and yet have no connection with other planes of existence, and therefore be valueless to those who are seeking to investigate those planes, therefore it is that the occultist pays great attention to the subjective aspect of his phenomena, because he knows how liable it is to falsify his results, and the initiate of an occult school is taught that he must know his own subconscious before he can function upon another plane, because he has always to go out *through* his subconscious on to that plane, and return by the same road, and unless he can correlate his conscious and subconscious minds, he will not be able to carry through his memory.

It frequently happens that a medium who is perfectly genuine may fail to pass beyond the subconscious level and will remain in a subjective state among his own subconscious wishes; in this light hypnoidal condition he will be peculiarly sensitive to the minds of the sitters and also to any mental currents that may be playing around him, or a secondary personality, often left over from childhood, may commence to function; this is a most unsatisfactory condition, and one that has brought much discredit upon trance phenomena because it can be so easily demonstrated that the phenomenon is purely subjective, and even the best mediums are liable to get entangled at the subconscious level if they are worried or upset, or out of harmony with their circle. The methods of psycho-analysis can easily demonstrate the material used to weave the phantasies of this level, which are built up in precisely the same manner as dreams, out of the medium's subconscious memories, but with this difference, that they are motivated, not only by his wishes and volitions, but also by those of the sitters, even if unexpressed, and therefore have a great psychological interest, although their objective and superphysical testimony is nil.

III. - Direct perception. Upon the hypothesis of telepathy the bulk of occult phenomena is built up. If we admit the possibility of a mind sending forth a thought which can affect another mind, then the whole structure of occult phenomena follows. We have enough evidence of telepathy for even the material scientist to accept nowadays, and a great many of them do. To what then does this theory lead? Upon this assumption we admit, in the first place, that a thought is a thing, formed by the mind and projected outside itself, that it is a manifestation of force, in its turn manifests force, and is capable of producing reactions under certain conditions. We conceive of thought as a form of force capable of objective activity.

The results of this admission must be very far-reaching. We cannot fail to be aware of the constant mental activity that goes on in all our minds, and if this be not confined to the mind of the thinker, but is projected into his environment, then that environment must undergo modification. Occultism has always held this to be so, but psychology has repudiated the assumption, root and branch, and when confronted with many well-authenticated cases, has answered them by hypotheses of subconscious seeing, hearing and remembering which, if we accept this explanation, confer upon the five physical senses powers quite as esoteric as those they repudiate, and leave us in doubt as to which theory does least violence to our commonsense.

Supposing, however, this theory of thought transference or telepathy be accepted as a working hypothesis by psychology, where will it lead us? To my mind, it can be of the greatest value in the domain of psycho-pathology, giving us a clue to many obscure derangements, for, in addition to the knowledge we already have of the internal defects to which mind is liable, it enables us to gauge the influence of certain environmental factors hitherto unsuspected, for it shows us the interplay of mind upon mind. That this is a most important factor no experienced psychoanalyst can deny, and especially is it the case in those cases which may be classed under the broad heading of the psycho-pathology of the family life, and which are generally known under the narrower term of the Oedipus complex, though to my mind this represents but one aspect of the problem. Here the problem of the child's reaction to parental authority is of profound importance, and if we study the matter solely from the subjective aspect of the patient's mind, I think we fail to do justice to the case; we should also investigate the influence the parent exerts upon the child, not only past, but present, and in the case of only or favourite children we often find a most unwholesome rapport existing between parent and child, which needs to be dealt with, not only from the aspect of the child's reaction, but also from that of the parent's action. The same condition can exist between friends, or business connections, or employer and employee. It is true that this condition can be alleviated by an analysis of childhood memories, because, according to my experience, the factor of suggestibility is usually determined by parental authority, and how far the childish attitude towards it has been carried forward into adult life. But wherever I have to deal with a case of pathological resentment of authority or discipline, and inability to get on with others, I find that if I explain to the patient the occult theory of thought-transference, and show him how to defend himself against it, it very quickly solves the problem.

I fully admit, however, that the factor of conscious suggestion, whether deliberate or otherwise, plays a great part in these transactions, also the subconscious reaction to a suppressed wish along sex lines; these factors have all to be considered, hence the importance of psychology and occultism working hand in hand and counterchecking each other.

The question of psychometry, or the detection of the ideas associated with an object or place, I cannot enter upon deeply here, for it involves the whole theory of the nature of thought and is of the profoundest interest; suffice to say, however, that although it is my belief that genuine psychometry exists, one can often show the subconscious phantasy-mechanisms which serve as a substitute if the psychic should not be working clearly. Perfect good faith, however, is not incompatible with this source of error, the psychic may faithfully describe the vision which rises before him, and yet it may be nothing but a dream-structure evolved by his subconscious, and clearly revealing, to those who know how to look for them, his own repressed wishes and anxieties.

The question of the psychic reading of the "Akashic" records is of absorbing interest. Herein it is claimed that the psychic can decipher the memory of nature and so reconstruct past scenes in the world's history, and several books exist that purport to contain the records derived from this source. Scott-Elliott's "Atlantis" is an excellent example of this type of work, and so is Steiner's "Atlantis and Lemuria."

Before this idea be dismissed with ignominy it may be as well to remind the reader that it is in entire accord with Jung's concept of a racial subconscious to which we all have access and upon which much of our behaviour is based.

IV. - With regard to the action of discarnate and disincarnating spirits, an hypothesis long familiar to occultism, I cannot enter here upon the evidence, but must merely say that if you accept the theory of the survival of bodily death (and it is a doctrine to which all Christians nominally subscribe, whatever their attitude may be towards its logical implications), then you must admit that there may be souls in existence which have not got bodies, and if you also admit the hypothesis of telepathy or thought-transference, then you must admit that if a mind can function apart from its physical vehicle during life, then it can continue to function apart from it after the connection is severed, providing it retains its organisation, as an entity, and it is one of the doctrines of the Christian faith that it does.

We now come to the problem of Thought-forms, as the occultist calls them, or thought-transference or telepathy, as the psychologist calls them if he condescends to think about the problem at all. Here we must depend upon experimental evidence, and there is much available, though we could do with more taken under test conditions, but be it remembered that practically the whole theory of the widespread phenomena of Christian Science and other forms of mental healing, whose existence no one can deny, is based upon the assumption of thought-transference, and therefore of the Thought-form.

It should also be observed in this connection, that suggestion and "rapport" could be set up between discarnate entities and the living, and may play their part in psychopathology.

V. - With regard to the doctrine of reincarnation, and its concomitant, Kharma, here we come to an extraordinarily interesting and important psychological point; in fact, it may be said to form one of the foundations of psychology. Are we to construct our doctrine upon the hypothesis of a single life? Is the mind to be regarded as deriving its pabulum from the short span between life and death? Or shall we take for our unit the reincarnating soul, and think, not in terms of an *incarnation,* but of an *evolution?* There is a profound difference between the two attitudes. I need hardly say that I subscribe to the latter, and work from that point of view. For me it has thrown profound light upon the problem of psychology. How, under the ordinary hypotheses, can we account for the innate disposition of a child, which begins to show itself within a few hours of birth to an acute observer? Science explains it by the theory of heredity, but it cannot explain one thing which must have struck other observers, namely, that the circumstances of a man's life seem to be appropriate to his character; that is to say, if he has some weakness, his environment will conspire to play upon it, not once, but repeatedly, and he will have opportunities of yielding to his fault which are not forthcoming for the average individual. I have been repeatedly struck by this fact in examining the life histories of the cases that pass through my hands, whether as actual patients undergoing medical treatment, or as those who wish to be analysed for the sake of self-culture and not for any remedial purpose.

Psychology cannot explain this phenomenon, but occultism can, and can also show how to overcome it on the hypothesis of Kharma, which teaches that our life experiences are for the payment of debts and the eradication or development of traits of character. Again, the doctrine of reincarnation shows us why an individual has a tendency towards one type of pathology and not another, it determines the particular form of atavism that forms the nucleus of this neurosis, and it also indicates the lines which the synthesis should follow.

I believe that the time will come when the psychologist will regard a training in the occult arts as part of his equipment or will at least employ a competent psychic just as he at present employs an analytical chemist, and will say to him, "Get me the Kharmic record of this case, so that I may discover the key to the character."

Clairvoyance is to the psychologist what the microscope is to the biologist, it enables him to see the structure he is studying. I have had a good deal to do with the training of psychoanalysts, and it has been my unvarying experience that the best psychotherapists have a streak of psychism in them, that is why the Kelt and the highly strung Jew make better psychologists than the average stolid Anglo-Saxon.

I believe that psychology is steadily being forced towards the occult standpoint, and that the present generation will see the theories of thought-transference and reincarnation incorporated among the body of orthodox scientific doctrines. How anyone who works upon the human mind can escape their significance is a mystery. I only know that to me they came as a flash of light upon the darkness. I had felt as if I stood in the centre of a small circle of illumination cast by scientific knowledge, and that the darkness of the unknown pressed in upon every side. A number of threads were placed in my hands, and I was bidden unravel them, but the ends thereof disappeared into the darkness, and those threads were human lives. I had come to the point when I felt I could no longer carry on my work as a medical analyst owing to the poor percentage of success that attended our efforts, when the doctrines of occultism were brought to my notice. Immediately on this realisation, the circle of light was widened, and I could trace the run of the threads; I could see whence they came and whither they were tending, and from the segment could calculate the circle.

I commend the occult doctrines to psychologists, not as natural laws, but as working hypotheses, asking them to take them in that spirit and see whither the facts will lead them. We should think nothing human as alien to us, and if the phenomena presented by the human mind resist the accepted classification of science, shall we amend our science or reject the evidence of our senses? No one who investigates the matter can doubt the existence of these phenomena, it is only those who have never seen them who repudiate them - the witness cannot do so. What an irony it is that when an eminent scientific man examines the evidence and pronounces in its favour, far from his dictum being accepted, as it would be upon any other subject, it is his reputation that suffers.

No fact can be subversive of the truth, and if this mass of data known as psychic phenomena should take its place in natural science, knowledge would be the richer.

INDEX

Adepti, 35
Age of Reason, 34
Akashic records, 189
Alchemists, 122
America, 54
Angels, 35, 84, 119-20
    Racial, Group and National, 25, 140, 152, 154, 155-6
Aquarian age, 34, 37, 38, 140
Archons, 35
Armistice Day, 152, 155
Astral Plane or Light, 89, 135, 162-4
Astrological symbols, 144
Atlantis, 105
Atlantis, 189
Atlantis and Lemuria, 189
Aura, 48, 53, 108, 109
Automatic writing, 182, 184-7
Bailey, Alice A., 141
Barlow, Katherine, 49
Bergson, Henri, 41, 181
Besant, Mrs., 52
Bethlehem, 158
Bismark, 154
Black Death, 154
Blavatsky, Madame, 40, 41, 60, 147
Body of Light, 89
Bond, Frederick Bligh, 148, 179
Boughton, Rutland, 158
B.P.S. Quarterly Transactions, 180
Brine, H.C., 49
Butler, W.E., 29
Cammell, Charles R., 29, 30, 33, 36-40, 57
Carstairs, David, 101, 147-56
Central Stillness, 145
Chalice Orchard, 49

Chichester, A., 49
Christ, 142
Christianity, 37, 141, 189
Christian Science, 34, 189
Circle working, 108, 109
Clairvoyance, 157-61, 190
    psychology of, 164-8, 182, 187-9
College of the Adepti, 135
Collegium Spiritum Sanctum, 135
Consecrating, 126
Cosmic Doctrine, The, 113, 145, 150, 151
Cosmic Law, 39
Cosmic Medium, 103
Crawford, J.W., 10
Crookes, Sir William, 10
Curtis Webb, Maiya, 92, 101
Darwin, 127
Death, multitudinous, 154
Dedicand, 131
Delphic Oracles, 41
Demons, 123-4, 126
De Valera, 48
Devil, 174
Djwal Khul, 141-2
Earth Soul, 102
Eastern Tradition, 41, 54, 140-1
Elder Brethren, 102
Ego, 64, 67, 68, 100, 171
Egypt, Ancient, 41, 105
Egyptian
    contacts, 51, 54
    Master, 144-5
    pylon, 97
Eidolon, 174
Elemental Grades, 133
Elementals, 106, 120-2, 142-4
English Master, the, 137-8

Erskine, Thomas, 147, 150
Esoteric Tradition, 35
Etheric double, 17-19, 125
Eucharist, 126, 142
Eva C., 184
Evans, Dr. Thomas Penry, 151
Fornario, Netta, 149
Fraternities, 132, 135
Freemasonry, 124
Freud, 179, 180
German Group Soul, 154
Glastonbury, 49, 101, 148, 151, 179
Gnomes, 122
Golden Bough, The 132
Golden Dawn, Hermetic Order of, 41, 45, 92, 147
Good Shepherd, sign of, 100
Greater Mysteries, 53, 59
Great Ones, 62
Great Unmanifest, 121
Great White Lodge, 59, 135
Great Work, 142-3
Greek Master, 145-7
Guild of the Master Jesus, 49, 56
Haw-haw, Lord, 48
Hell, 22
Hilarion, 139
Higher consciousness, 174-8
Higher Self, 24, 25, 64, 67, 93, 103, 153
High Priest, 105
Hindu, 173-4
Hypnogogics, 90
Illuminati, 132
"Imperator", 36, 40, 128
India, 54
Individuality, 23, 65, 68
Inner Light Magazine, 28, 56, 86, 92, 128
Inner Light, Society (and Fraternity) of the, 28, 40, 58-62, 101, 105, 128, 136, 179
International Institute, 50
Introduction to Ritual Magic, An, 152
Isis Unveiled, 40
Jerusalem, 38
Joan of Arc, 84

John the Divine, St., 119
Kharma, 134, 182, 190
King Arthur, 56
Leadbeater, C.W., 60
Leukemia, 55
Lesser Mysteries, 53, 173
Light, 29, 39, 56, 57, 58
Lhasa, 38
Lodge, Sir Oliver, 10
Logoi, 186
London, 38, 40, 151
London (Royal Free Hospital) School of Medicine for Women, 179
Lord of Civilisation, 139
Lords of Flame, Form and Mind, 120-1, 155
Lords of Humanity, 25, 120
Loveday, C.T., 100, 148
Lower Self, 64, 67
Lumley Brown, Margaret, 56
Machinery of the Mind, The, 179
Magic, 133
Magnetising, 125
Mahatma Letters to A.P.Sinnett, The, 40, 41
Mann, Mrs. R., 49
Marylebone Spiritualist Association, 50, 56
Masters, 26, 55, 59, 60, 84, 94, 95, 96, 99, 100, 101, 102, 103, 121, 128-56
Master, Unnamed, 36-40, 56
Mathers, MacGregor, 41, 60, 105, 147
Maya, 162, 163
McDougal, Professor, 180
Mediumship explained from Beyond, 40
Methuen, Mrs., 50-55
Modus Operandi of Trance Communications, 57
Moll, Dr. Albert, 76
Monthly Letters, 56, 57, 58
More, Thomas, 147
Moriarty, Dr. Theodore, 92
Moses, Stainton, 40, 128
Mysteries, Ancient, 45
Mystery Schools, 32, 37, 80, 129-32

Index

Mystical Qabalah, The, 132
Napoleon, 103
Nature Spirits, 122-3
New Testament, 39
Newton, Sir Isaac, 80
Nuremberg trials, 153
Oath of the Mysteries, 62
Occult Movement, 36
"Old Greek, the," 113, 114, 150
Old Testament, 32, 84
Osiris, 17, 18, 21, 22, 24, 26
Owen, Vale, 119
Personality, 23, 24, 65, 67, 68, 142-3
Physical phenomena, 182, 183-4
Piscean Age, 34, 37, 155
Plan, 142-3
Planes, 12-13, 172-4
Prince, Dr. Morton, 83
Psychic Science, 180
Psychic Studies, College of, 39, 180
Psychism, 133, 157-78, 182, 187-9
    Astral, 161-4
Psychoanalysis, 80, 179, 185, 188, 191
Psychology and Occultism, 180-91
Psychometry, 188
Purgatory, 22
Pythagoras, 150
Pythoness, 101, 103-115
Qabalah, 119
Qlipphoth, 120, 123-4, 126
Rainbow Bridge, 144
Rakoczi, 139-41
Ray, 111
Rays and the Initiations, The, 141
Reincarnation, 8-12, 182, 190
Return of Arthur, The, 56
Rome, 38
Sairey Gamp, 26
Salamanders, 122
Salpêtrière, 96-7
Scatcherd, Miss, 184
Schizophrenia, 68, 90
Scott-Elliott, 189
Scribe, 106-108
Second Death, 23, 25
Secret Chiefs, 147

Secret Doctrine, The, 132
Secret Tradition, The, 41-49
Secret Wisdom, 33
Seeker, 130
Self, 68
Serapis, 142-4
Shakespeare, 158
Shalott, Lady of, 157
"Silver Birch", 128
Society for Psychical Research, 181
Solar Logos, 121
Spence, Lewis, 56
Spirit, 142-4, 177-8
Spiritualism in the Light of Occult Science, 28, 58
Spiritualist Movement, 33, 34, 35, 58-62
Steiner, Rudolf, 189
Supernals, 143
Swedenborgian movement, 35
Sylphs, 122
Symbol system, 132
Tansley, A.G., 179
Taverner, Dr., 92
Tschiffeling's Ride, 98
Thebes, 38
Theosophical Society, 34, 41, 52
Thought Forms, 124-6, 189
Thomas á Becket, 147
Through the Gates of Death, 28, 58
Tibet, 41
Tibetan Master, 141
Tibetan spirits, 51
Trance,
    desirable conditions for, 30
    hypnotic, 75-79, 86, 89
    Mediumistic, 67, 68, 89, 92-7
    mental phenomena of, 72-75
    modus operandi of, 31-2
    of Projection, 67, 73, 86, 89, 90, 91, 92
    of Vision, 67, 73, 86, 89, 90, 92
    physical phenomena of, 69-72
    Problem of, The, 86-92
    psychology of, 63-8
    speaking, 182, 184-7
    technique of, 79-85, 102-115

Tranchell Hayes, Maiya, 92
Triangle working, 108, 109
Tyler, Mack, 149
Undines, 122
University of London, 179
Virgin Mary, 84
Vision, 169-72
War criminals, 152
Weekly Letters, 56
Western Tradition, 41, 53, 140-1
Wheel of Birth and Death, 134
"White Eagle", 128
"White Wing", 50-55
Witch trials of Middle Ages, 41
Words of the Masters, 92
World Teacher, 52
World War, First, 34, 154, 179
World War, Second, 155
Yoga, 45
Ypres, 147

Other titles from Thoth Publications

AN INTRODUCTION TO RITUAL MAGIC
By Dion Fortune & Gareth Knight

At the time this was something of a unique event in esoteric publishing - a new book by the legendary Dion Fortune. Especially with its teachings on the theory and practice of ritual or ceremonial magic, by one who, like the heroine of two of her other novels, was undoubtedly "a mistress of that art".

In this work Dion Fortune deals in successive chapters with Types of Mind Working; Mind Training; The Use of Ritual; Psychic Perception; Ritual Initiation; The Reality of the Subtle Planes; Focusing the Magic Mirror; Channelling the Forces; The Form of the Ceremony; and The Purpose of Magic - with appendices on Talisman Magic and Astral Forms.

Each chapter is supplemented and expanded by a companion chapter on the same subject by Gareth Knight. In Dion Fortune's day the conventions of occult secrecy prevented her from being too explicit on the practical details of magic, except in works of fiction. These veils of secrecy having now been drawn back, Gareth Knight has taken the opportunity to fill in much practical information that Dion Fortune might well have included had she been writing today.

In short, in this unique collaboration of two magical practitioners and teachers, we are presented with a valuable and up-to-date text on the practice of ritual or ceremonial magic "as it is". 'That is to say, as a practical, spiritual, and psychic discipline, far removed from the lurid superstition and speculation that are the hall mark of its treatment in sensational journalism and channels of popular entertainment.

ISBN 1-870450 31 0 Deluxe Hardback Limited edition
ISBN 1-870450 26 4 Soft cover edition

THE CIRCUIT OF FORCE
by Dion Fortune.
With commentaries by Gareth Knight.

In "The Circuit of Force", Dion Fortune describes techniques for raising the personal magnetic forces within the human aura and their control and direction in magic and in life, which she regards as 'the Lost Secrets of the Western Esoteric Tradition'.

To recover these secrets she turns to three sources.

a) the Eastern Tradition of Hatha Yoga and Tantra and their teaching on raising the "sleeping serpent power" or kundalini;

b) the circle working by means of which spiritualist seances concentrate power for the manifestation of some of their results;

c) the linking up of cosmic and earth energies by means of the structured symbol patterns of the Qabalistic Tree of Life.

Originally produced for the instruction of members of her group, this is the first time that this material has been published for the general public in volume form.

Gareth Knight provides subject commentaries on various aspects of the etheric vehicle, filling in some of the practical details and implications that she left unsaid in the more secretive esoteric climate of the times in which she wrote.

Some quotes from Dion Fortune's text:

"When, in order to concentrate exclusively on God, we cut ourselves off from nature, we destroy our own roots. There must be in us a circuit between heaven and earth, not a one-way flow, draining us of all vitality. It is not enough that we draw up the Kundalini from the base of the spine; we must also draw down the divine light through the Thousand-Petalled Lotus. Equally, it is not enough for out mental health and spiritual development that we draw down the Divine Light, we must also draw up the earth forces. Only too often mental health is sacrificed to spiritual development through ignorance of, or denial of, this fact."

"....the clue to all these Mysteries is to be sought in the Tree of Life. Understand the significance of the Tree; arrange the symbols you are working with in the correct manner upon it, and all is clear and you can work out your sum. Equate the Danda with the Central Pillar, and the Lotuses with the Sephiroth and the bi-sections of the Paths thereon, and you have the necessary bilingual dictionary at your disposal - if you known how to use it."

ISBN 1-870450 28 0   Soft cover edition

PRINCIPLES OF HERMETIC PHILOSOPHY
& The Esoteric Philosophy of Astrology

Principles of Hermetic Philosophy together with *The Esoteric Philosophy of Astrology* are the last known works written by Dion Fortune. They appeared in her Monthly letters to members and associates of the Society of the Inner Light between November 1942 and March 1944.

Her intention in these works is summed up in her own words: "The observation in these pages are an attempt to gather together the fragments of a forgotten wisdom and explain and expand them in the light of personal observation."

She was uniquely equipped to make highly significant personal observations in these matters as one of the leading practical occultists of her time. What is more, in these later works she feels less constrained by traditions of occult secrecy and takes an altogether more practical approach than in her earlier, well known textbooks.

Gareth knight takes the opportunity to amplify her explanations and practical exercises with a series of full page illustrations, and provides a commentary on her work, together with a further three chapters on recent practical work in the Hermetic Tradition.

ISBN 1-870450-34-5

*   *   *   *   *

THE STORY OF DION FORTUNE
As told to Charles Fielding and Carr Collins.

Dion Fortune and Aleister Crowley stand as the twentieth century's most influential leaders of the Western Esoteric Tradition. They were very different in their backgrounds, scholarship and style.

But, for many, Dion Fortune is the chosen exemplar of the Tradition - with no drugs, no homosexuality and no kinks. This book tells of her formative years and of her development.

At the end, she remains a complex and enigmatic figure, who can only be understood in the light of the system she evolved and worked to great effect.

There can be no definitive "Story of Dion Fortune". This book must remain incompete and full of errors. However, readers may find themselves led into an experience of initiation as envisaged by this fearless and dedicated woman.

ISBN 1-870450-33-7

PRACTICAL MAGIC AND THE WESTERN MYSTERY TRADITION
Unpublished Essays and Articles by W. E. Butler.

W. E. Butler, a devoted friend and colleague of the celebrated occultist Dion Fortune, was among those who helped build the Society of the Inner Light into the foremost Mystery School of its day. He then went on to found his own school, the Servants of the Light, which still continues under the guidance of Dolores Ashcroft-Nowicki, herself an occultist and author of note and the editor and compiler of this volume.

PRACTICAL MAGIC AND THE WESTERN TRADITION is a collection of previously unpublished articles, training papers, and lectures covering many aspects of practical magic in the context of western occultism that show W. E. Butler not only as a leading figure in the magical tradition of the West, but also as one of its greatest teachers.

Subjects covered include:

What makes an Occultist
Ritual Training
Inner Plane Contacts and Rays
The With Cult
Keys in Practical Magic
Telesmatic Images
Words of Power
An Explanation of Some Psychic Phenomena

ISBN 1-870450-32-9